D1320713

The Pleasures of Walking

THE PLEASURES
OF WALKING

EDITED BY

EDWIN VALENTINE MITCHELL

NEW YORK · THE VANGUARD PRESS, INC.

THE PLEASURES OF WALKING

INTRODUCTORY NOTE

W HEN I REMARKED TO A
friend that I was engaged in compiling an anthology on
the subject of walking, he said, "I suppose the depressed
state of the world has made walkers of a great many people
who a few years ago were almost in danger of losing the
use of their legs. It's odd, when you stop to think of it,
that because of the harshness of the times and the fact that
shoe leather is cheaper than gasoline a lot of people have
been driven to the discovery that walking is among the
most rewarding pleasures of life."

This commentary gave me the hint that perhaps I should
include in this collection something by or concerning
those who have been walkers through sheer necessity
rather than by choice. It accounts, in fact, for the presence
among these reprints of George Gissing's reminiscences of
walks in London and also for Charles Dickens' observations of those wayside tatterdemalions whom every walker
meets, because such characters are always to be found
slog-footing it along the roads of every land.

One kind of walking which I do not recall seeing men-
tioned anywhere in the literature of the subject is imaginary walking. When I asked Mr. John Finley if I might
use his essay, "Traveling Afoot," which originally appeared
a number of years ago in the old *Outlook,* he said in his

letter granting me leave to do so, "You may be interested to know that I have a little game that I play alone: namely, that of walking in some other part of the world as many miles as I actually walk here day by day, with the result that I have walked nearly 20,000 miles here in the last six years, which means that I have covered the land part of the earth in a circuit of the globe. I finished last night 2,000 miles since the first of January 1934 and in doing so reached Vancouver from the north. My first year's walk was across the United States and I then started on the west coast of France. I will not bother you now with the rest of the itinerary but tell you only that I crossed Europe, southern Asia and then up through China and parts farther north to Bering Strait and from Alaska down to Vancouver."

To those who may look in these pages for practical advice concerning the paraphernalia of walking, such as footgear, rucksacks, and clothing, all I can say is that I interviewed a veteran walker with a view to the possibility of getting something of the sort for the book, but about the only advice of any kind he was willing to impart was this: "Ladies should not walk alone in Corsica."

JOHN FINLEY:
TRAVELING AFOOT

"TRAVELING AFOOT" — THE
very words start the imagination out upon the road! One's
nomad ancestors cry within one across centuries and invite
to the open spaces. Many to whom this cry comes are im-
pelled to seek the mountain paths, the forest trails, the
solitudes or wildernesses coursed only by the feet of wild
animals. But to me the black or dun roads, the people's
highways, are the more appealing — those strips or ribbons
of land which is still held in common, the paths wide
enough for the carriages of the rich and the carts of the
poor to pass each other, the roads over which they all bear
their creaking burdens or run on errands of mercy or
need, but preferably roads that do not also invite the flying automobiles, whose occupants so often make the
pedestrian feel that even these strips have ceased to be
democratic.

My traveling afoot, for many years, has been chiefly in
busy city streets or in the country roads into which they
run — not far from the day's work or from the thorough-
fares of the world's concerns.

Of such journeys on foot which I recall with greatest
pleasure are some that I have made in the encircling of
cities. More than once I have walked around Manhattan

Island (an afternoon's or a day's adventure within the reach of thousands), keeping as close as possible to the water's edge all the way round. One not only passes through physical conditions illustrating the various stages of municipal development from the wild forest at one end of the island to the most thickly populated spots of the earth at the other, but one also passes through diverse cities and civilizations. Another journey of this sort was one that I made around Paris, taking the line of the old fortifications, which are still maintained, with a zone following the fortifications most of the way just outside, inhabited only by squatters, some of whose houses were on wheels ready for "mobilization" at an hour's notice. (It was near the end of that circumvallating journey, about sunset, on the last day of an old year, that I saw my first airplane rising like a great golden bird in the aviation field, and a few minutes later my first elongated dirigible — precursors of the air armies.)

I have read that the Scots once had a custom of making a yearly pilgrimage or excursion around their boroughs or cities — "beating the bounds," they called it, following the boundaries that they might know what they had to defend. It is a custom that might profitably be revived. We should then know better the cities in which we live. We should be stronger, healthier, for such expeditions, and the better able and the more willing to defend our boundaries.

But these are the exceptional foot expeditions. For most urbanites there is the opportunity for the daily walk to and from work, if only they were not tempted by the wheel of the street car or motor. During the subway strike in New York not long ago I saw able-bodied men riding in improvised barges or buses going at a slower-than-walking pace, because, I suppose, though still possessed of legs, these cliff dwellers had become enslaved by wheels, just like the old mythical Ixion who was tied to one.

I once walked late one afternoon with a man who did not know that he could walk, from the Custom-House, down near the Battery, to the City College gymnaisum, 138th Street, and what we did (at the rate of a mile in about twelve minutes) thousands are as able to do, though not perhaps at this pace when the streets are full.

And what a "preparedness" measure it would be if thousands of the young city men would march uptown every day after hours, in companies! The swinging stride of a companionless avenue walk, on the other hand, gives often much of the adventure that one has in carrying the ball in a football game.

Many times when I could not get out of the city for a vacation I have walked up Fifth Avenue at the end of the day and have half closed my eyes in order to see men and women as the blind man saw them when his eyes were first touched by the Master — see them as "trees walk-ing."

But the longing of all at times, whether it be an atavistic or a cultivated longing, is for the real trees and all that goes with them. Immediately there open valleys with "pitcher" elms, so graceful that one thinks of the famous

line from the *Odyssey* in which Ulysses says that once
he saw a tree as beautiful as the most beautiful woman —
valleys with elms, hill-tops with far-signaling poplars,
mountains with pines, or prairies with their groves and
orchards. About every city lies an environing charm, even
if it have no trees, as, for example, Cheyenne, Wyoming,
where, stopping for a few hours not long ago, I spent
most of the time walking out to the encircling mesas that
give view of both mountains and city. I have never found a
city without its walkers' rewards. New York has its Pali-
sade paths, its Westchester hills and hollows, its "south
shore" and "north shore," and its Staten Island (which
I have often thought of as Atlantis, for once on a holiday
I took Plato with me to spend an afternoon on its littoral,
away from the noise of the city, and on my way home
found that my Plato had stayed behind, and he never
reappeared, though I searched car and boat). Chicago
has its miles of lake shore walks; Albany, its Helderbergs;
and San Francisco, its Golden Gate Road. And I recall
with a pleasure which the war cannot take away a number
of suburban European walks. One was across the Cam-
pagna from Frascati to Rome, when I saw an Easter week
sun go down behind the Eternal City. Another was out to
Fiesole from Florence and back again; another, out and
up from where the Saône joins the Rhône at Lyons; another, from Montesquieu's château to Bordeaux; another,
from Edinburgh out to Arthur's Seat and beyond; another, from Lausanne to Geneva, past Paderewski's villa,
along the glistening lake with its background of Alps;

and still another, from Eton (where I spent the night in a cubicle looking out on Windsor Castle) to London, starting at dawn. One cannot know the intimate charm of the urban penumbra who makes only shuttle journeys by motor or street cars.

These are near journeys, but there are times when they do not satisfy, when one must set out on a far journey, test one's will and endurance of body, or get away from the usual. Sometimes the long walk is the only medicine. Once when suffering from one of the few colds of my life (incurred in California) I walked from the rim of the Grand Canyon of the Colorado down to the river and back (a distance of fourteen miles, with a descent of five thousand feet and a like ascent), and found myself entirely cured of the malady which had clung to me for days. My first fifty-mile walk years ago was begun in despair over a slow recovery from the sequelæ of diphtheria.

But most of these far walks have been taken just for the joy of walking in the free air. Among these have been journeys over Porto Rico (of two hundred miles), around Yellowstone Park (of about one hundred and fifty miles, making the same stations as the coaches), over portages along the waterways following the French explorers from the Gulf of St. Lawrence to the Gulf of Mexico, and in country roads visiting one-room schools in the State of New York and over the boundless prairie fields long ago.

But the walks which I most enjoy, in retrospect at any rate, are those taken at night. Then one makes one's own landscape with only the help of the moon or stars or the distant lights of a city, or with one's unaided imagination if the sky is filled with cloud.

The next better thing to the democracy of a road by day is the monarchy of a road by night, when one has one's own terrestrial way under guidance of a Providence that is nearer. It was in the "cool of the day" that the Almighty is pictured as walking in the garden, but I have most often met him on the road by night.

Several times I have walked down Staten Island and across New Jersey to Princeton "after dark," the destination being a particularly attractive feature of this walk. But I enjoy also the journeys that are made in strange places where one knows neither the way nor the destination, except from a map or the advice of signboard or kilometer posts (which one reads by the flame of a match, or, where that is wanting, sometimes by following the letters and figures on a post with one's fingers) , or the information, usually inaccurate, of some other wayfarer. Most of these journeys have been made of a necessity that has prevented my making them by day, but I have in every case been grateful afterward for the necessity. In this country they have been usually among the mountains — the Green Mountains or the White Mountains or the Catskills. But of all my night faring, a night on the moors of Scotland is the most impressive and memorable, though without incident. No mountain landscape is to me more awesome than the moorlands by night, or more alluring than the moorlands by day when the

☆ *14* ☆

heather is in bloom. Perhaps this is only the ancestors speaking again.

But something besides ancestry must account for the others. Indeed, in spite of it, I was drawn one night to Assisi, where St. Francis had lived. Late in the evening I started on to Foligno in order to take a train in to Rome for Easter morning. I followed a white road that wound around the hills, through silent clusters of cottages tightly shut up with only a slit of light visible now and then, meeting not a human being along the way save three somber figures accompanying an ox cart, a man at the head of the oxen and a man and woman at the tail of the cart — a theme for Millet. (I asked in broken Italian how far it was to Foligno, and the answer was, *"Una hora"* — distance in time and not in miles.) Off in the night I could see the lights of Perugia, and some time after midnight I began to see the lights of Foligno — of Perugia and Foligno, where Raphael had wandered and painted. The adventure of it all was that when I reached Foligno I found that it was a walled town, that the gate was shut, and that I had neither passport nor intelligible speech. There is an interesting walking sequel to this journey. I carried that night a wooden water-bottle, such as the Italian soldiers used to carry, filling it from the fountain at the gate of Assisi before starting. Just a month later, under the same full moon, I was walking between midnight and morning in New Hampshire. I had the same water-bottle and stopped at a spring to fill it. When I turned the bottle upside down, a few drops of water from the fountain of Assisi fell into the New England spring, which for me, at any rate, has been forever sweetened by this association.

All my long night walks seem to me now as but preparation for one which I was obliged to make at the outbreak of the war in Europe. I had crossed the Channel from England to France, on the day that war was declared by England, to get a boy of ten years out of the war zone. I got as far by rail as a town between Arras and Amiens, where I expected to take a train on a branch road toward Dieppe; but late in the afternoon I was informed that the scheduled train had been canceled and that there might not be another for twenty-four hours, if then. Automobiles were not to be had even if I had been able to pay for one. So I set out at dusk on foot toward Dieppe, which was forty miles or more distant. The experiences of that night would in themselves make one willing to practice walking for years in order to be able to walk through such a night in whose dawn all Europe waked to war. There was the quiet, serious gathering of the soldiers at the place of rendezvous; there were the all-night preparations of the peasants along the way to meet the new conditions; there was the pelting storm from which I sought shelter in the niches for statues in the walls of an abandoned château; there was the clatter of the hurrying feet of soldiers or gendarmes who properly arrested the wanderer, searched him, took him to a guardhouse, and detained him until certain that he was an American citizen and a friend of France, when he was let go on his way with a *"Bon voyage"*; there was the never-to-be-forgotten dawn upon the harvest fields in which only old men, women, and children were at work; there was the gathering of the peasants with commandeered horses and carts in the beautiful park on the water-front at Dieppe; and there was much besides; but they were experiences for the most part which only one on foot could have had.

And the moral of my whole story is that walking is not only a joy in itself, but that it gives an intimacy with the sacred things and the primal things of earth that are not revealed to those who rush by on wheels.

I have wished to organize just one more club — the "Holy Earth" club, with the purposes that Liberty Bailey has set forth in his book of the same title (*The Holy Earth*), but I should admit to membership in it (except for special reasons) only those who love to walk upon the earth.

Traveling afoot! This is the best posture in which to worship the God of the Out-of-Doors!

LESLIE STEPHEN:

IN PRAISE OF WALKING

THE DAY ON WHICH I WAS
fully initiated into the mysteries is marked by a white
stone. It was when I put on a knapsack and started from
Heidelberg for a march through the Odenwald. Then I
first knew the delightful sensation of independence and
detachment enjoyed during a walking tour. Free from all
bothers of railway timetables and extraneous machinery,
you trust to your own legs, stop when you please, diverge
into any track that takes your fancy, and drop in upon
some quaint variety of human life at every inn where
you put up for the night. You share for the time the mood
in which Borrow settled down in the dingle after escaping
from his bondage in the publishers' London slums. You
have no dignity to support, and the dress-coat of conven-
tional life has dropped into oblivion, like the bundle from
Christian's shoulders. You are in the world of Lavengro,
and would be prepared to take tea with Miss Isopel
Berners or with the Welsh preacher who thought that he

had committed the unpardonable sin. Borrow, of course, took the life more seriously than the literary gentleman who is only escaping on ticket-of-leave from the prison-house of respectability, and is quite unequal to a personal conflict with "blazing-Bosville" — the flaming tinman. He is only dipping in the element where his model was thoroughly at home. I remember, indeed, one figure in that first walk which I associate with Benedict Moll, the strange treasure-seeker whom Borrow encountered in his Spanish rambles. My acquaintance was a mild German innkeeper, who sat beside me on a bench while I was trying to assimilate certain pancakes, the only dinner he could provide, still fearful in memory, but just attackable after a thirty-mile tramp. He confided to me that, poor as he was, he had discovered the secret of perpetual motion. He kept his machine upstairs, where it discharged the humble duty of supplying the place of a shoeblack; but he was about to go to London to offer it to a British capitalist. He looked wistfully at me as possibly a capitalist in (very deep) disguise, and I thought it wise to evade a full explanation. I have not been worthy to encounter many of such quaint incidents and characters as seem to have been normal in Borrow's experience; but the first walk, commonplace enough, remains distinct in my memory. I kept no journal, but I could still give the narrative day by day — the sights which I dutifully admired and the very state of my bootlaces. Walking tours thus rescue a bit of one's life from oblivion. They play in one's personal recollections the part of those historical passages in which

☆ *19* ☆

LESLIE STEPHEN : *In Praise of Walking*

Carlyle is an unequalled master; the little islands of light
in the midst of the darkening gloom of the past, on
which you distinguish the actors in some old drama actually alive and moving. The devotee of other athletic
sports remembers special incidents: the occasion on which
he hit a cricket-ball over the pavilion at Lord's, or the
crab which he caught as his boat was shooting Barnes
Bridge. But those are memories of exceptional moments
of glory or the reverse, and apt to be tainted by vanity or
the spirit of competition. The walks are the unobtrusive
connecting thread of other memories, and yet each walk
is a little drama itself, with a definite plot with episodes
and catastrophes, according to the requirements of Aris-
totle; and it is naturally interwoven with all the thoughts,
the friendships, and the interests that form the staple of
ordinary life.

Walking is the natural recreation for a man who desires
not absolutely to suppress his intellect but to turn it out
to play for a season. All great men of letters have, therefore, been enthusiastic walkers (exceptions, of course, ex-
cepted). Shakespeare, besides being a sportsman, a lawyer,
a divine, and so forth, conscientiously observed his own
maxim, "Jog on, jog on, the footpath way"; though a full
proof of this could only be given in an octavo volume.
Anyhow, he divined the connection between walking and
a "merry heart"; that is, of course, a cheerful acceptance
of our position in the universe, founded upon the deepest
moral and philosophical principles. His friend Ben Jonson
walked from London to Scotland. Another gentleman of

the period (I forget his name) danced from London to Norwich. Tom Coryate hung up in his parish church the shoes in which he walked from Venice and then started to walk (with occasional lifts) to India. Contemporary walkers of more serious character might be quoted, such as the admirable Barclay, the famous Quaker apologist, from whom the great Captain Barclay inherited his prowess. Every one, too, must remember the incident in Walton's *Life of Hooker*. Walking from Oxford to Exeter, Hooker went to see his godfather, Bishop Jewel, at Salisbury. The bishop said that he would lend him "a horse which hath carried me many a mile, and, I thank God, with much ease," and "presently delivered into his hands a walking-staff with which he professed he had travelled through many parts of Germany." He added ten groats and munificently promised ten groats more when Hooker should restore the "horse." When, in later days, Hooker once rode to London, he expressed more passion than that mild divine was ever known to show upon any other occasion against a friend who had dissuaded him from "footing it." The hack, it seems, "trotted when he did not," and discomposed the thoughts which had been soothed by the walking-staff. His biographer must be counted, I fear, among those who do not enjoy walking without the incidental stimulus of sport. Yet the "Compleat Angler" and his friends start by a walk of twenty good miles before they take their "morning draught." Swift, perhaps, was the first person to show a full appreciation of the moral and physical advantages of walking.

LESLIE STEPHEN : *In Praise of Walking*

He preached constantly upon this text to Stella, and practised his own advice. It is true that his notions of a journey were somewhat limited. Ten miles a day was his regular allowance when he went from London to Holyhead, but then he spent time in lounging at wayside inns to enjoy the talk of the tramps and ostlers. The fact, though his biographers are rather scandalised, shows that he really appreciated one of the true charms of pedestrian expeditions. Wesley is generally credited with certain moral reforms, but one secret of his power is not always noticed. In his early expeditions he went on foot to save horse-hire, and made the great discovery that twenty or thirty miles a day was a wholesome allowance for a healthy man. The fresh air and exercise put "spirit into his sermons," which could not be rivalled by the ordinary parson of the period, who too often passed his leisure lounging by the fire-side. Fielding points the contrast. Trulliber, embodying the clerical somnolence of the day, never gets beyond his pigsties, but the model Parson Adams steps out so vigorously that he distances the stage-coach, and disappears in the distance rapt in the congenial pleasures of walking and composing a sermon. Fielding, no doubt, shared his hero's taste, and that explains the contrast between his vigorous naturalism and the sentimentalism of Richardson, who was to be seen, as he tells us, "stealing along from Hammersmith to Kensington with his eyes on the ground, propping his unsteady limbs with a stick." Even the ponderous Johnson used to dissipate his early hypochondria by walking from Lichfield to Birmingham and back (thirty-two miles), and his later melancholy would have changed to a more cheerful view of life could he have kept up the practice in his beloved London streets. The literary movement at the end of the eighteenth century was obviously due in great part, if not mainly, to the renewed practice of walking. Wordsworth's poetical autobiography shows how every stage in his early mental development was connected with some walk in the Lakes. The sunrise which startled him on a walk after a night spent in dancing first set him apart as a "dedicated spirit." His walking tour in the Alps — then a novel performance — roused him to his first considerable poem. His chief performance is the record of an excursion on foot. He kept up the practice, and De Quincey calculated somewhere what multiple of the earth's circumference he had measured on his legs, assuming, it appears, that he averaged ten miles a day. De Quincey himself, we are told, slight and fragile as he was, was a good walker, and would run up a hill "like a squirrel." Opium-eating is not congenial to walking, yet even Coleridge, after beginning the habit, speaks of walking forty miles a day in Scotland, and, as we all know, the great manifesto of the new school of poetry, the "Lyrical Ballads," was suggested by the famous walk with Wordsworth, when the first stanzas of the "Ancient Mariner" were composed. A remarkable illustration of the wholesome influence might be given from the cases of Scott and Byron. Scott, in spite of his lameness, delighted in walks of twenty and thirty miles a day, and in climbing crags, trusting to the strength of his arms to remedy the stumblings of his foot. The early strolls enabled him to saturate his mind with local traditions, and the passion for walking under difficulties showed the manly nature, which has endeared him to three generations. Byron's lameness was too severe to admit of walking, and therefore all the unwholesome humours which would have been walked off in a good cross-country march accumulated in his brain and caused the defects, the morbid affectation and perverse misanthropy, which half ruined the achievement of the most masculine intellect of his time.

It is needless to accumulate examples of a doctrine which will no doubt be accepted as soon as it is announced. Walking is the best of panaceas for the morbid tendencies of authors. It is, I need only observe, as good for reasoners as for poets. The name "peripatetic" suggests the connection. Hobbes walked steadily up and down the hills in his patron's park when he was in his venerable old age. To the same practice may be justly ascribed the utilitarian philosophy. Old Jeremy Bentham kept himself up to his work for eighty years by his regular "post-jentacular circumgyrations." His chief disciple, James Mill, walked incessantly and preached as he walked. John Stuart Mill imbibed at once psychology, political economy, and a love of walks from his father. Walking was his one recreation; it saved him from becoming a mere smoke-dried pedant; and though he put forward the pretext of botanical researches, it helped him to perceive that man is something besides a mere logic machine. Mill's great rival as a spiritual guide, Carlyle, was a vigorous walker, and even in his latest years was a striking figure when performing his regular constitutionals in London. One of the vivid passages in the *Reminiscences* describes his walk with Irving from Glasgow to Drumclog. Here they sat on the "brow of a peat hag, while far, far away to the westward, over our brown horizon, towered up white and visible at the many miles of distance a high irregular pyramid. Ailsa Craig we at once guessed, and thought of the seas and oceans over yonder." The vision naturally led to a solemn conversation, which was an event in both lives. Neither Irving nor Carlyle himself feared any amount of walking in those days, it is added, and next Carlyle took his longest walk, fifty-four miles. Carlyle is unsurpassable in his discriptions of scenery: from the pictures of mountains in *Sartor Resartus* to the battle-pieces in *Frederick*. Ruskin, himself a good walker, is more rhetorical but not so graphic; and it is self-evident that nothing educates an eye for the features of a landscape so well as the practice of measuring it by your own legs.

The great men, it is true, have not always acknowledged their debt to the genuis, whoever he may be, who presides over pedestrian exercise. Indeed, they have inclined to ignore the true source of their impulse. Even when they speak of the beauties of nature, they would give us to understand that they might have been disembodied spirits, taking aerial flights among mountain solitudes, and independent of the physical machinery of legs and stomachs. When long ago the Alps cast their spell upon me, it was woven in a great degree by the eloquence of *Modern Painters.* I hoped to share Ruskin's ecstasies in a reverent worship of Mont Blanc and the Matterhorn. The influence of any cult, however, depends upon the character of the worshipper, and I fear that in this case the charm operated rather perversely. It stimulated a passion for climbing which absorbed my energies and distracted me from the prophet's loftier teaching. I might have followed him from the mountains to picture-galleries, and spent among the stones of Venice hours which I devoted to attacking hitherto unascended peaks and so losing my last chance of becoming an art critic. I became a fair judge of an Alpine guide, but I do not even know how to make a judicious allusion to Botticelli or Tintoretto. I can't say that I feel the smallest remorse. I had a good time, and at least escaped one temptation to talking nonsense. It follows, however, that my passion for the mountains had something earthly in its composition. It is associated with memories of eating and drinking. It meant delightful comradeship with some of the best friends; but our end, I admit, was not always of the most exalted or æsthetic strain. A certain difficulty results. I feel an uncomfortable diffidence. I hold that Alpine walks are the poetry of the pursuit; I could try to justify the opinion by relating some of the emotions suggested by the great scenic effects: the sunrise on the snow fields; the storm-clouds gathering under the great peaks; the high pasturages knee-deep in flowers; the torrents plunging through the "cloven ravines," and so forth. But the thing has been done before, better than I could hope to do it; and when I look back at those old passages in *Modern Painters,* and think of the enthusiasm which prompted to exuberant sentences of three and four hundred words, I am not only abashed by the thought of their unapproachable eloquence, but feel as though they conveyed a tacit reproach. You, they seem to say, are, after all, a poor prosaic creature, affecting a love of sublime scenery as a cloak for more grovelling motives. I could protest against this judgment, but it is better at present to omit the topic, even though it would give the strongest groundwork for my argument.

Perhaps, therefore, it is better to trust the case for walking to where the external stimulus of splendours and sublimities is not so overpowering. A philosophic historian divides the world into the regions where man is stronger than nature and the regions where nature is stronger than man. The true charm of walking is most unequivocally shown when it is obviously dependent upon the walker himself. I became an enthusiast in the Alps, but I have found almost equal pleasure in walks such as one described by Cowper, where the view from a summit is bounded, not by Alps or Apennines, but by "a lofty quickset hedge." Walking gives a charm to the most commonplace British scenery. A love of walking not only makes any English county tolerable but seems to make the charm inexhaustible. I know only two or three districts minutely, but the more familiar I have become with any one of them the more I have wished to return to invent some new combination of old strolls or to inspect some hitherto unexplored nook. I love the English Lakes, and certainly not on account of associations. I cannot "associate." Much as I respect Wordsworth, I don't care to see the cottage in which he lived: it only suggests to me that anybody else might have lived there. There is an intrinsic charm about the Lake Country, and to me at least a music in the very names of Helvellyn and Skiddaw and Scawfell. But this may be due to the suggestion that it is a miniature of the Alps. I appeal, therefore, to the Fen Country, the country of which Alton Locke's farmer boasted that it had none of your "darned ups and downs" and "was as flat as his barn-door for forty miles on end." I used to climb the range of the Gogmagogs, to see the tower of Ely, some sixteen miles across the dead level, and I boasted that every term I devised a new route for walking to the cathedral from Cambridge. Many of these routes led by the little public-house called "Five Miles from Anywhere": which in my day was the Mecca to which a remarkable club, called — from the name of the village — the "Upware Republic," made periodic pilgrimages. What its members specifically did when they got there beyond consuming beer is unknown to me; but the charm was in the distance "from anywhere" — a sense of solitude under the great canopy of the heavens, where, like emblems of infinity,

The trenchèd waters run from sky to sky.

I have always loved walks in the Fens. In a steady march along one of the great dykes by the monotonous canal with the exuberant vegetation dozing in its stagnant waters, we were imbibing the spirit of the scenery. Our talk might be of senior wranglers or the University crew, but we felt the curious charm of the great flats. The absence, perhaps, of definite barriers makes you realise that you are on the surface of a planet rolling through free and boundless space. One queer figure comes back to me — a kind of scholar-gipsy of the fens. Certain peculiarities made it undesirable to trust him with cash, and his family used to support him by periodically paying his score at riverside publics. They allowed him to print certain poems, moreover, which he would impart when one met him on the towpath. In my boyhood, I remember, I used to fancy that the most delightful of all lives must be that of a bargee — enjoying a perpetual picnic. This gentleman seemed to have carried out the idea; and in the intervals of lectures I could fancy that he had chosen the better part. His poems, alas! have long vanished from my memory, and I therefore cannot quote what would doubtless have given the essence of the local sentiment and invested such names as Wicken Fen or Swaffham Lode with associations equal to those of Arnold's Hincksey ridge and Fyfield elm.

Another set of walks may, perhaps, appeal to more general sympathy. The voice of the sea, we know, is as powerful as the voice of the mountains; and, to my taste, it is difficult to say whether the Land's End is not in itself a more impressive station than the top of Mont Blanc. The solitude of the frozen peaks suggests tombstones and death. The sea is always alive and at work. The hovering gulls and plunging gannets and the rollicking porpoises are animating symbols of a gallant struggle with wind and wave. Even the unassociative mind has a vague sense of the Armada and Hakluyt's heroes in the background. America and Australia are just over the way. "Is not this a dull place?" asked some one of an old woman whose cottage was near to the Lizard lighthouse. "No," she replied, "it is so 'cosmopolitan'." That was a simple-minded way of expressing the charm suggested in Milton's wonderful phrase ——

Where the great Vision of the guarded Mount
Looks towards Namancos and Bayona's hold.

She could mentally follow the great ships coming and going, and shake hands with people at the ends of the earth. The very sight of a fishing-boat, as painters seem to have found out, is a poem in itself. But is it not all written in *Westward Ho!* and in the *Prose Idylls,* in which Kingsley put his most genuine power? Of all walks that I have made, I can remember none more delightful than those round the southwestern promotory. I have followed the coast at different times from the mouth of the Bristol Avon by the Land's End to the Isle of Wight, and I am only puzzled to decide which bay or cape is the most delightful. I only know that the most delightful was the more enjoyable when placed in its proper setting by a long walk. When you have made an early start, followed the coastguard track on the slopes above the cliffs, struggled through the gold and purple carpeting of gorse and heather on the moors, dipped down into quaint little coves with a primitive fishing village, followed the blinding whiteness of the sands round a lonely bay, and at last emerged upon a headland where you can settle into a nook of the rocks, look down upon the glorious blue of the Atlantic waves breaking into foam on the granite, and see the distant sea-levels glimmering away till they blend imperceptibly into cloudland; then you can consume your modest sandwiches, light your pipe, and feel more virtuous and thoroughly at peace with the universe than it is easy even to conceive yourself elsewhere. I have fancied myself on such occasions to be a felicitous blend of poet and saint — which is an agreeable sensation. What I wish to point out, however, is that the sensation is confined to the walker. I respect the cyclist, as I have said; but he is enslaved by his machine: he has to follow the highroad, and can only come upon what points of view open to the commonplace tourist. He can see nothing of the retired scenery which may be close to him, and cannot have his mind brought into due harmony by the solitude and by the long succession of lovely bits of scenery which stand so coyly aside from the public notice.

The cockney cyclist, who wisely seeks to escape at intervals from the region "where houses thick and sewers annoy the air," suffers the same disadvantages. To me, for many years, it was a necessity of life to interpolate gulps of fresh air between the periods of inhaling London fogs. When once beyond the "town," I looked out for notices that trespassers would be prosecuted. That gave a strong presumption that the trespass must have some attraction. The cyclist could only reflect that trespassing for him was not only forbidden but impossible. To me it was a reminder of the many delicious bits of walking which, even in the neighbourhood of London, await the man who has no superstitious reverence for legal rights. It is indeed surprising how many charming walks can be contrived by a judicious combination of a little trespassing with the rights of way happily preserved over so many commons and footpaths. London, it is true, goes on stretching its vast octopus arms farther into the country. Unlike the devouring dragon of Wantley, to whom "houses and churches" were like "geese and turkies," it spreads houses and churches over the fields of our childhood. And yet, between the great lines of railway there are still fields not yet desecrated by advertisements of liver pills. It is a fact that within twenty miles of London two travellers recently asked their way at a lonely farmhouse; and that the mistress of the house, seeing that they were far from an inn, not only gave them a seat and luncheon, but positively refused to accept payment. That suggested an idyllic state of society which, it is true, one must not count upon discovering. Yet hospitality, the virtue of primitive regions, has not quite vanished, it would appear, even from this over-civilised region. The travellers, perhaps, had something specially attractive in their manners. In that or some not distant ramble they made time run back for a couple of centuries. They visited the quiet grave where Penn lies under the shadow of the old Friends' meetinghouse, and came to the cottage where the seat on which Milton talked to Ellwood about *Paradise Regained* seems to be still waiting for his return; and climbed the hill to the queer monument with records how Captain Cook demonstrated the goodness of Providence by disproving the existence of a continent in the South Sea — (the argument is too obvious to require exposition) ; and then gazed reverently upon the obelisk, not far off, which marks the point at which George III concluded a famous stag hunt. A little valley in the quiet chalk country of Buckinghamshire leads past these and other memorials, and the lover of historical associations, with the help of Thorne's *Environs of London,* may add indefinitely to the list. I don't object to an association when it presents itself spontaneously and unobstrusively. It should not be the avowed goal but the accidental addition to the interest of a walk; and it is then pleasant to think of one's ancestors as sharers in the pleasures. The region enclosed within a radius of thirty miles from Charing Cross has charms enough even for the least historical of minds. You cannot hold a fire in your hand, according to a high authority, by thinking on the frosty Caucasus; but I can comfort myself now and then, when the fellow-passengers who tread on my heels in London have put me out of temper, by thinking of Leith Hill. It only rises to the height of a thousand feet by help of the "Folly" on the top, but you can see, says my authority, twelve counties from the tower; and, if certain legendary ordnance surveyors spoke the truth, distinguish the English Channel to the south, and Dunstable Hill, far beyond London, to the north. The Crystal Palace, too, as we are assured, "sparkles like a diamond." That is gratifying; but to me the panorama suggests a whole network of paths, which have been the scene of personally conducted expeditions, in which I displayed the skill on which I most pride myself — skill, I mean, in devising judicious geographical combinations, and especially of contriving admirable short cuts. The persistence of some companions in asserting that my short cuts might be the longest way round shows that the best of men are not free from jealousy. Mine, at any rate, led me and my friends through pleasant places innumerable. My favourite passage in *Pilgrim's Progress* — an allegory which could have occurred, by the way, to no one who was not both a good man and a good walker — was always that in which Christian and Hopeful leave the highroad to cross a stile into "Bypath Meadow." I should certainly have approved the plan. The path led them, it is true, into the castle of Giant Despair; but the law of trespass has become milder; and the incident really added that spice of adventure which is delightful to the genuine pilgrim. We defied Giant Despair; and if our walks were not quite so edifying as those of Christian and his friends, they add a pleasant strand to the thread of memory which joins the past years. Conversation, we are often told, like letter-writing, is a lost art. We live too much in crowds. But if ever men can converse pleasantly, it is when they are invigorated by a good march: when the reserve is lowered by the long familiarity of a common pursuit, or when, if bored, you can quietly drop behind, or perhaps increase the pace sufficiently to check the breath of the persistent argufier.

Nowhere, at least, have I found talk flow so freely and

pleasantly as in a march through pleasant country. And yet there is also a peculiar charm in the solitary expedition when your interlocutor must be yourself. That may be enjoyed, perhaps even best enjoyed, in London streets themselves. I have read somewhere of a distinguished person who composed his writings during such perambulations, and the statement was supposed to prove his remarkable power of intellectual concentration. My own experience would tend to diminish the wonder. I hopelessly envy men who can think consecutively under conditions distracting to others — in crowded meeting or in the midst of their children — for I am as sensitive as most people to distraction; but if I can think at all, I am not sure that the roar of the Strand is not a more favourable environment than the quiet of my own study. The mind — one must only judge from one's own — seems to me to be a singularly ill-constructed apparatus. Thoughts are slippery things. It is terribly hard to keep them in the track presented by logic. They jostle each other, and suddenly skip aside to make room for irrelevant and accidental neighbours; till the stream of thought, of which people talk, resembles rather such a railway journey as one makes in dreams, where at every few yards you are shunted on to the wrong line. Now, though a London street is full of distractions, they become so multitudinous that they neutralise each other. The whirl of conflicting impulses becomes a continuous current because it is so chaotic and determines a mood of sentiment if not a particular vein of reflection. Wordsworth describes the influence upon himself in a curious passage of his *Prelude*. He wandered through London as a raw country lad, seeing all the sights from Bartholomew Fair to St. Stephen's, and became a unit of the "monstrous ant-hill in a too busy world." Of course, according to his custom, he drew a moral, and a most excellent moral, from the bewildering complexity of his new surroundings. He learned, it seems, to recognise the unity of man and to feel that the spirit of nature was upon him "in London's vast domain" as well as on the mountains. That comes of being a philosophical poet with a turn for optimism. I will not try to interpret or to comment, for I am afraid that I have not shared the emotions which he expresses. A cockney, born and bred, takes surroundings for granted. The hubbub has ceased to distract him; he is like the people who were said to become deaf because they always lived within the roar of a waterfall: he realises the common saying that the deepest solitude is solitude in a crowd; he derives a certain stimulus from a vague sympathy with the active life around him, but each particular stimulus remains, as the phrase goes, "below the threshold of consciousness." To some such effect, till psychologists will give me a better theory, I attribute the fact that what I please to call my "mind" seems to work more continuously and coherently in a street walk than elsewhere. This, indeed, may sound like a confession of cynicism. The man who should open his mind to the impressions naturally suggested by the "monstrous ant-hill" would be in danger of becoming a philanthropist or a pessimist, of being overpowered by thoughts of gi-

gantic problems, or of the impotence of the individual
to solve them. Carlyle, if I remember rightly, took Emer-
son round London in order to convince his optimistic
friend that the devil was still in full activity. The gates
of hell might be found in every street. I remember how,
when coming home from a country walk on a sweltering
summer night, and seeing the squalid population turning
out for a gasp of air in their only playground, the vast
labyrinth of hideous lanes, I seemed to be in Thomson's
"City of Dreadful Night." Even the vanishing of quaint
old nooks is painful when one's attention is aroused.
There is a certain churchyard wall, which I pass sometimes, with an inscription to commemorate the benefactor
who erected it "to keep out the pigs." I regret the pigs
and the village green which they presumably imply. The
heart, it may be urged, must be hardened not to be moved
by many such texts for melancholy reflection. I will not
argue the point. None of us can be always thinking over
the riddle of the universe, and I confess that my mind is
generally employed on much humbler topics. I do not
defend my insensibility nor argue that London walks
are the best. I only maintain that even in London walking
has a peculiar fascination. The top of an omnibus is an
excellent place for meditation; but it has not, for me at
least, that peculiar hypnotic influence which seems to be
favourable to thinking and to pleasant day-dreaming when
locomotion is carried on by one's own muscles. The charm,
however, is that even a walk in London often vaguely
recalls better places and nobler forms of the exercise.

Wordsworth's Susan hears a thrush at the corner of Wood
Street, and straightway sees

A mountain ascending, a vision of trees,
Bright volumes of vapour through Lothbury glide
And a river flows on through the vale of Cheapside

The gulls which seem lately to have found out the
merits of London give to occasional Susans, I hope, a
whiff of fresh sea-breezes. But, even without gulls or wood-
pigeons, I can often find occasions in the heart of London
for recalling the old memories, without any definable
pretext; little pictures of scenery, sometimes assignable
to no definable place, start up invested with a faint aroma
of old friendly walks and solitary meditations and strenu-
ous exercise, and I feel convinced that, if I am not a
thorough scoundrel, I owe that relative excellence to the
harmless monomania which so often took me, to appropriate Bunyan's phrase, from the amusements of Vanity
Fair to the Delectable Mountains of pedestrianism.

MAX BEERBOHM:

GOING OUT FOR A WALK

It IS A FACT THAT NOT ONCE
in all my life have I gone out for a walk. I have been taken
out for walks; but that is another matter. Even while I
trotted prattling by my nurse's side I regretted the good
old days when I had, and wasn't a perambulator. When I
grew up it seemed to me that the one advantage of living
in London was that nobody ever wanted me to come out
for a walk. London's very drawbacks — its endless noise
and hustle, its smoky air, the squalor ambushed everywhere
in it — assured this one immunity. Whenever I was with
friends in the country, I knew that at any moment, unless
rain were actually falling, some man might suddenly say,
"Come out for a walk!" in that sharp imperative tone
which he would not dream of using in any other connection. People seem to think there is something inherently
noble and virtuous in the desire to go for a walk. Any one
thus desirous feels that he has a right to impose his will on
whomever he sees comfortably settled in an arm-chair,
reading. It is easy to say simply "No" to an old friend. In
the case of a mere acquaintance one wants some excuse. "I
wish I could, but" — nothing ever occurs to me except "I
have some letters to write." This formula is unsatisfactory
in three ways. (1) It isn't believed. (2) It compels you to

rise from your chair, go to the writing-table, and sit improvising a letter to somebody until the walkmonger (just not daring to call you liar and hypocrite) shall have lumbered out of the room. (3) It won't operate on Sunday mornings. "There's no post out till this evening" clinches the matter; and you may as well go quietly.

Walking for walking's sake may be as highly laudable and exemplary a thing as it is held to be by those who practise it. My objection to it is that it stops the brain. Many a man has professed to me that his brain never works so well as when he is swinging along the high road or over hill and dale. This boast is not confirmed by my memory of anybody who on a Sunday morning has forced me to partake of his adventure. Experience teaches me that whatever a fellow-guest may have of power to instruct or to amuse when he is sitting on a chair, or standing on a hearth-rug, quickly leaves him when he takes one out for a walk. The ideas that came so thick and fast to him in any room, where are they now? where that encyclopædic knowledge which he bore so lightly? where the kindling fancy that played like summer lightning over any topic that was started? The man's face that was so mobile is set now; gone is the light from his fine eyes. He says that A. (our host) is a thoroughly good fellow. Fifty yards further on, he adds that A. is one of the best fellows he has ever met. We tramp another furlong or so, and he says that Mrs. A. is a charming woman. Presently he adds that she is one of the most charming women he has ever known. We pass an inn. He reads vapidly aloud to me: "The King's Arms. Licensed to sell Ales and Spirits." I foresee that during the rest of the walk he will read aloud any inscription that occurs. We pass a "Uxminster. 11 Miles." We turn a sharp corner at the foot of a hill. He points at the wall, and says "Drive Slowly." I see far ahead, on the other side of the hedge bordering the high road, a small notice-board. He sees it too. He keeps his eye on it. And in due course "Trespassers," he says, "Will Be Prosecuted." Poor man! — mentally a wreck.

Luncheon at the A.'s, however, salves him and floats him in full sail. Behold him once more the life and soul of the party. Surely he will never, after the bitter lesson of this morning, go out for another walk. An hour later, I see him striding forth, with a new companion. I watch him out of sight. I know what he is saying. He is saying that I am rather a dull man to go a walk with. He will presently add that I am one of the dullest men he ever went a walk with. Then he will devote himself to reading out the inscriptions.

How comes it, this immediate deterioration in those who go walking for walking's sake? Just what happens? I take it that not by his reasoning faculties is a man urged to this enterprise. He is urged, evidently, by something in him that transcends reason; by his soul, I presume. Yes, it must be the soul that raps out the "Quick march!" to the body. — "Halt! Stand at ease!" interposes the brain, and "To what destination," it suavely asks the soul, "and on what errand, are you sending the body?" — "On no errand whatsoever," the soul makes answer, "and to no destination at all. It is just like you to be always on the look-out for some subtle ulterior motive. The body is going out because the mere fact of its doing so is a sure indication of nobility, probity, and rugged grandeur of character." — "Very well, Vagula, have your own wayula! But I," says the brain, "flatly refuse to be mixed up in this tomfoolery. I shall go to sleep till it is over." The brain then wraps itself up in its own convolutions, and falls into a dreamless slumber from which nothing can rouse it till the body has been safely deposited indoors again.

Even if you go to some definite place, for some definite purpose, the brain would rather you took a vehicle; but it does not make a point of this; it will serve you well enough unless you are going for a walk. It won't, while your legs are vying with each other, do any deep thinking for you, nor even any close thinking; but it will do any number of small odd jobs for you willingly — provided that your legs, also, are making themselves useful, not merely bandying you about to gratify the pride of the soul. Such as it is, this essay was composed in the course of a walk, this morning. I am not one of those extremists who must have a vehicle to every destination. I never go out of my way, as it were, to avoid exercise. I take it as it comes, and take it in good part. That valetudinarians are always chattering about it, and indulging in it to excess, is no reason for despising it. I am inclined to think that in moderation it is rather good for one, physically. But, pending a time when no people wish me to go and see them, and I have no wish to go and see any one, and there is nothing whatever for me to do off my own premises, I never will go out for a walk.

CHARLES DICKENS:

NIGHT WALKS

SOME YEARS AGO, A TEMPO-
rary inability to sleep, referable to a distressing impression,
caused me to walk about the streets all night, for a series
of several nights. The disorder might have taken a long
time to conquer, if it had been faintly experimented on
in bed; but it was soon defeated by the brisk treatment of
getting up directly, after lying down, and going out, and
coming home tired at sunrise.

In the course of those nights, I finished my education
in a fair amateur experience of houselessness. My principal
object being to get through the night, the pursuit of it
brought me into sympathetic relations with people who
have no other object every night in the year.

The month was March, and the weather damp, cloudy,
and cold. The sun not rising before half-past five, the night
perspective looked sufficiently long at half-past twelve;
which was about my time for confronting it.

The restlessness of a great city, and the way in which it
tumbles and tosses before it can get to sleep, formed one
of the first entertainments offered to the contemplation of
us houseless people. It lasted about two hours. We lost a
great deal of companionship when the late public-houses
turned their lamps out, and when the potmen thrust the

last brawling drunkards into the street; but stray vehicles and stray people were left us, after that. If we were very lucky, a policeman's rattle sprang and a fray turned up; but, in general, surprisingly little of this diversion was provided. Except in the Haymarket, which is the worst kept part of London, and about Kent-street in the Borough, and along a portion of the line of the Old Kent-road, the peace was seldom violently broken. But, it was always the case that London, as if in imitation of individual citizens belonging to it, had expiring fits and starts of restlessness. After all seemed quiet, if one cab rattled by, half-a-dozen would surely follow; and Houselessness even observed that intoxicated people appeared to be magnetically attracted towards each other; so that we knew when we saw one drunken object staggering against the shutters of a shop, that another drunken object would stagger up before five minutes were out, to fraternise or fight with it. When we made a divergence from the regular species of drunkard, the thin-armed, puff-faced, leaden-lipped gin-drinker, and encountered a rarer specimen of a more decent appearance, fifty to one but that specimen was dressed in soiled mourning. As the street experience in the night, so the street experience in the day; the common folk who come unexpectedly into a little property come unexpectedly into a deal of liquor.

At length these flickering sparks would die away, worn out — the last veritable sparks of waking life trailed from some late pieman or hot-potato man — and London would sink to rest. And then the yearning of the houseless mind

☆ *44* ☆

would be for any sign of company, any lighted place, any movement, anything suggestive of any one being up — nay, even so much as awake, for the houseless eye looked out for lights in windows.

Walking the streets under the pattering rain, Houselessness would walk and walk and walk, seeing nothing but the interminable tangle of streets, save at a corner, here and there, two policemen in conversation, or the sergeant or inspector looking after his men. Now and then in the night — but rarely — Houselessness would become aware of a furtive head peering out of a doorway a few yards before him, and, coming up with the head, would find a man standing bolt upright to keep within the doorway's shadow, and evidently intent upon no particular service to society. Under a kind of fascination, and in a ghostly silence suitable to the time, Houselessness and this gentleman would eye one another from head to foot, and so, without exchange of speech, part, mutually suspicious. Drip, drip, drip, from ledge and coping, splash from pipes and water-spouts, and by-and-by the houseless shadow would fall upon the stones that pave the way to Waterloo-bridge; it being in the houseless mind to have a halfpenny worth of excuse for saying "Good-night" to the toll-keeper, and catching a glimpse of his fire. A good fire and a good great-coat and a good woollen neck-shawl, were comfortable things to see in conjunction with the toll-keeper; also his brisk wakefulness was excellent company when he rattled the change of halfpence down upon that metal table of his, like a man who defied the night, with all its sorrowful thoughts, and didn't care for the coming of dawn. There was need of encouragement on the threshold of the bridge, for the bridge was dreary. The chopped-up murdered man had not been lowered with a rope over the parapet when those nights were; he was alive, and slept then quietly enough most likely, and undisturbed by any dream of where he was to come. But the river had an awful look, the buildings on the banks were muffled in black shrouds, and the reflected lights seemed to originate deep in the water, as if the spectres of suicides were holding them to show where they went down. The wild moon and clouds were as restless as an evil conscience in a tumbled bed, and the very shadow of the immensity of London seemed to lie oppressively upon the river.

Between the bridge and the two great theatres, there was but the distance of a few hundred paces, so the theatres came next. Grim and black within, at night, those great dry Wells, and lonesome to imagine, with the rows of faces faded out, the lights extinguished, and the seats all empty. One would think that nothing in them knew itself at such a time but Yorick's skull. In one of my night walks, as the church steeples were shaking the March winds and rain with strokes of Four, I passed the outer boundary of one of these great deserts, and entered it. With a dim lantern in my hand, I groped my well-known way to the stage and looked over the orchestra — which was like a great grave dug for a time of pestilence — into the void beyond. A dismal cavern of an immense aspect, with the chandelier gone dead like everything else, and nothing visible through mist and fog and space, but tiers of winding-sheets. The ground at my feet where, when last there, I had seen the peasantry of Naples dancing among the vines, reckless of the burning mountain which threatened to overwhelm them, was now in possession of a strong serpent of engine-hose, watchfully lying in wait for the serpent Fire, and ready to fly at it if it showed its forked tongue. A ghost of a watchman, carrying a faint corpse candle, haunted the distant upper gallery and flitted away. Retiring within the proscenium, and holding my light above my head towards the rolled-up curtain — green no more, but black as ebony — my sight lost itself in a gloomy vault, showing faint indications in it of a shipwreck of canvas and cordage. Methought I felt much as a diver might, at the bottom of the sea.

In those small hours when there was no movement in the streets, it afforded matter for reflection to take Newgate in the way, and, touching its rough stone, to think of the prisoners in their sleep, and then to glance in at the lodge over the spiked wicket, and see the fire and light of the watching turnkeys, on the white wall. Not an inappropriate time either, to linger by that wicked little Debtors' Door — shutting tighter than any other door one ever saw — which has been Death's Door to so many. In the days of the uttering of forged one-pound notes by people tempted up from the country, how many hundreds of wretched creatures of both sexes — many quite innocent — swung out of a pitiless and inconsistent world, with the tower of yonder Christian church of Saint Sepulchre monstrously before their eyes! Is there any haunting of the Bank Parlour, by the remorseful souls of old directors, in the nights of these later days, I wonder, or is it as quiet as this degenerate Aceldama of an Old Bailey?

To walk on the Bank, lamenting the good old times and bemoaning the present evil period, would be an easy next step, so I would take it, and would make my houseless circuit of the Bank, and give a thought to the treasure within; likewise to the guard of soldiers passing the night there, and nodding over the fire. Next, I went to Billingsgate, in some hope of market-people, but it proving as yet too early, crossed London-bridge and got down by the waterside on the Surrey shore among the buildings of the great brewery. There was plenty going on at the brewery; and the reek, and the smell of grains, and the rattling of the plump dray horses at their mangers, were capital company. Quite refreshed by having mingled with this good society, I made a new start with a new heart, setting the old King's Bench prison before me for my next object, and resolving, when I should come to the wall, to think of poor Horace Kinch, and the Dry Rot in men.

A very curious disease the Dry Rot in men, and difficult to detect the beginning of. It had carried Horace Kinch inside the wall of the old King's Bench prison, and it had carried him out with his feet foremost. He was a likely man to look at, in the prime of life, well to do, as clever as he needed to be, and popular among many friends. He was suitably married, and had healthy and pretty children.

But, like some fair-looking houses or fair-looking ships, he took the Dry Rot. The first strong external revelation of the Dry Rot in men, is a tendency to lurk and lounge; to be at street-corners without intelligible reason; to be going anywhere when met; to be about many places rather than at any; to do nothing tangible, but to have an intention of performing a variety of intangible duties tomorrow or the day after. When this manifestation of the disease is observed, the observer will usually connect it with a vague impression once formed or received, that the patient was living a little too hard. He will scarcely have had leisure to turn it over in his mind and form the terrible suspicion "Dry Rot," when he will notice a change for the worse in the patient's appearance: a certain slovenliness and deterioration, which is not poverty, nor dirt, nor intoxication, nor ill-health, but simply Dry Rot. To this, succeeds a smell of strong waters, in the morning; to that, a looseness respecting money; to that, a stronger smell as of strong waters, at all times; to that, a looseness respecting everything; to that, a trembling of the limbs, somnolency, misery, and crumbling to pieces. As it is in wood, so it is in men. Dry Rot advances at a compound usury quite incalculable. A plank is found infected with it, and the whole structure is devoted. Thus it had been with the unhappy Horace Kinch, lately buried by a small subscription. Those who knew him had not nigh done saying, "So well off, so comfortably established, with such hope before him — and yet, it is feared, with a slight touch of Dry Rot!" when lo! the man was all Dry Rot and dust.

DICKENS : *Night Walks*

From the dead wall associated on those houseless nights with this too common story, I chose next to wander by Bethlehem Hospital; partly, because it lay on my road round to Westminster; partly, because I had a night fancy in my head which could be best pursued within sight of its walls and dome. And the fancy was this: Are not the sane and the insane equal at night as the sane lie a dreaming? Are not all of us outside this hospital, who dream, more or less in the condition of those inside it, every night of our lives? Are we not nightly persuaded, as they daily are, that we associate preposterously with kings and queens, emperors and empresses, and notabilities of all sorts? Do we not nightly jumble events and personages and times and places, as these do daily? Are we not sometimes troubled by our own sleeping inconsistencies, and do we not vexedly try to account for them or excuse them, just as these do sometimes in respect of their waking delusions? Said an afflicted man to me, when I was last in a hospital like this, "Sir, I can frequently fly." I was half ashamed to reflect that so could I — by night. Said a woman to me on the same occasion, "Queen Victoria frequently comes to dine with me, and her Majesty and I dine off peaches and macaroni in our night-gowns, and his Royal Highness the Prince Consort does us the honour to make a third on horseback in a Field-Marshal's uniform." Could I refrain from reddening with consciousness when I remembered the amazing royal parties I myself had given (at night), the unaccountable viands I had put on table, and my extraordinary manner of con-

☆ *50* ☆

ducting myself on those distinguished occasions? I wonder that the great master who knew everything, when he called Sleep the death of each day's life, did not call Dreams the insanity of each day's sanity.

By this time I had left the Hospital behind me, and was again setting towards the river; and in a short breathing space I was on Westminster-bridge, regaling my houseless eyes with the external walls of the British Parliament — the perfection of a stupendous institution, I know, and the admiration of all surrounding nations and succeeding ages, I do not doubt, but perhaps a little the better now and then for being pricked up to its work. Turning off into Old Palace-yard, the Courts of Law kept me company for a quarter of an hour; hinting in low whispers what numbers of people they were keeping awake, and how intensely wretched and horrible they were rendering the small hours to unfortunate suitors. Westminster Abbey was fine gloomy society for another quarter of an hour; suggesting a wonderful procession of its dead among the dark arches and pillars, each century more amazed by the century following it than by all the centuries going before. And indeed in those houseless night walks — which even included cemeteries where watchmen went round among the graves at stated times, and moved the tell-tale handle of an index which recorded that they had touched it at such an hour — it was a solemn consideration what enormous hosts of dead belong to one old great city, and how, if they were raised while the living slept, there would not be the space of a pin's point in all the streets and ways for the living to come out into. Not only that, but the vast armies of dead would overflow the hills and valleys beyond the city, and would stretch away all round it, God knows how far.

When a church clock strikes, on houseless ears in the dead of the night, it may be at first mistaken for company and hailed as such. But, as the spreading circles of vibration, which you may perceive at such a time with great clearness, go opening out, for ever and ever afterwards widening perhaps (as the philosopher has suggested) in eternal space, the mistake is rectified and the sense of loneliness is profounder. Once — it was after leaving the Abbey and turning my face north — I came to the great steps of St. Martin's church as the clock was striking Three. Suddenly, a thing that in a moment more I should have trodden upon without seeing, rose up at my feet with a cry of loneliness and houselessness, struck out of it by the bell, the like of which I never heard. We then stood face to face looking at one another, frightened by one another. The creature was like a beetle-browed hair-lipped youth of twenty, and it had a loose bundle of rags on, which it held together with one of its hands. It shivered from head to foot, and its teeth chattered, and as it stared at me — persecutor, devil, ghost, whatever it thought me — it made with its whining mouth as if it were snapping at me, like a worried dog. Intending to give this ugly object money, I put out my hand to stay it — for it recoiled as it whined and snapped — and laid my hand upon its shoulder. Instantly, it twisted out of its garment, like the young man in the New Testament, and left me standing alone with its rags in my hands.

Covent-garden Market, when it was market morning, was wonderful company. The great waggons of cabbages, with growers' men and boys lying asleep under them, and with sharp dogs from market-garden neighbourhoods looking after the whole, were as good as a party. But one of the worst night sights I know in London, is to be found in the children who prowl about this place; who sleep in the baskets, fight for the offal, dart at any object they think they can lay their thieving hands on, dive under the carts and barrows, dodge the constables, and are perpetually making a blunt pattering on the pavement of the Piazza with the rain of their naked feet. A painful and unnatural result comes of the comparison one is forced to institute between the growth of corruption as displayed in the so much improved and cared for fruits of the earth, and the growth of corruption as displayed in these all uncared for (except inasmuch as everhunted) savages.

There was early coffee to be got about Covent-garden Market, and that was more company — warm company, too, which was better. Toast of a very substantial quality, was likewise procurable; though the towzled-headed man who made it, in an inner chamber within the coffee-room, hadn't got his coat on yet, and was so heavy with sleep that in every interval of toast and coffee he went off anew behind the partition into complicated cross-roads of choke and snore, and lost his way directly. Into one of these establishments (among the earliest) near Bow-street, there came one morning as I sat over my houseless cup, pondering where to go next, a man in a high and long snuff-coloured coat, and shoes, and, to the best of my belief, nothing else but a hat, who took out of his hat a large cold meat pudding; a meat pudding so large that it was a very tight fit, and brought the lining of the hat out with it. This mysterious man was known by his pudding, for on his entering, the man of sleep brought him a pint of hot tea, a small loaf, and a large knife and fork and plate. Left to himself in his box, he stood the pudding on the bare table, and, instead of cutting it, stabbed it, overhand, with the knife, like a mortal enemy; then took the knife out, wiped it on his sleeve, tore the pudding asunder with his fingers, and ate it all up. The remembrance of this man with the pudding remains with me as the remembrance of the most spectral person my houselessness encountered. Twice only was I in that establishment, and twice I saw him stalk in (as I should say, just out of bed, and presently going back to bed), take out his pudding, stab his pudding, wipe the dagger, and eat his pudding all up. He was a man whose figure promised cadaverousness, but who had an excessively red face, though shaped like a horse's. On the second occasion of my seeing him, he said huskily to the man of sleep, "Am I red to-night?" "You are," he uncompromisingly answered. "My mother," said the spectre, "was a red-faced woman that liked drink, and I looked at her hard when she laid in her coffin, and I took the complexion." Somehow, the pudding seemed an unwholesome pudding after that, and I put myself in its way no more.

When there was no market, or when I wanted variety, a railway terminus with the morning mails coming in, was remunerative company. But like most of the company to be had in this world, it lasted only a very short time. The station lamps would burst out ablaze, the porters would emerge from places of concealment, the cabs and trucks would rattle to their places (the post-office carts were already in theirs), and, finally, the bell would strike up, and the train would come banging in. But there were few passengers and little luggage, and everything scuttled away with the greatest expedition. The locomotive post-offices, with their great nets — as if they had been dragging the country for bodies — would fly open as to their doors, and would disgorge a smell of lamp, an exhausted clerk, a guard in a red coat, and their bags of letters; the engine would blow and heave and perspire, like an engine wiping its forehead and saying what a run it had had; and within ten minutes the lamps were out, and I was houseless and alone again.

But now, there were driven cattle on the high road near, wanting (as cattle always do) to turn into the midst of stone walls, and squeeze themselves through six inches' width of iron railing, and getting their heads down (also as cattle always do) for tossing-purchase at quite imaginary dogs, and giving themselves and every devoted creature associated with them a most extraordinary amount of unnecessary trouble. Now, too, the conscious gas began to grow pale with the knowledge that daylight was coming, and straggling work-people were already in the streets, and, as waking life had become extinguished with the last pieman's sparks, so it began to be rekindled with the fires of the first street-corner breakfast-sellers. And so by faster and faster degrees, until the last degrees were very fast, the day came, and I was tired and could sleep. And it is not, as I used to think, going home at such times, the least wonderful thing in London, that in the real desert region of the night, the houseless wanderer is alone there. I knew well enough where to find Vice and Misfortune of all kinds, if I had chosen; but they were put out of sight, and my houselessness had many miles upon miles of streets in which it could, and did, have its own solitary way.

— From *The Uncommercial Traveller.*

F 2

GEORGE MACAULAY TREVELYAN:
WALKING

I HAVE TWO DOCTORS, MY LEFT
leg and my right. When body and mind are out of gear
(and those twin parts of me live at such close quarters
that the one always catches melancholy from the other)
I know that I shall have only to call in my doctors and I
shall be well again.

Mr. Arnold Bennett has written a religious tract called
The Human Machine. Philosophers and clergymen are
always discussing why we should be good — as if any one
doubted that he ought to be. But Mr. Bennett has tackled
the real problem of ethics and religion — how we can make
ourselves be good. We all of us know that we ought to be
cheerful to ourselves and kind to others, but cheerfulness
is often, and kindness sometimes, as unattainable as sleep
in a white night. That combination of mind and body
which I call my soul is often so choked up with bad
thoughts or useless worries, that

> "Books and my food, and summer rain,
> Knock on my sullen heart in vain."

It is then that I call in my two doctors to carry me off
for the day.

Mr. Bennett's recipe for the blue devils is different.

He proposes a course of mental "Swedish exercises," to develop by force of will the habit of "concentrating thought" away from useless angers and obsessions and directing it into clearer channels. This is good, and I hope that every one will read and practise Mr. Bennett's precepts. It is good, but it is not all. For there are times when my thoughts, having been duly concentrated on the right spot, refuse to fire, and will think nothing except general misery; and such times, I suppose, are known to all of us.

On these occasions my recipe is to go for a long walk. My thoughts start out with me like blood-stained mutineers debauching themselves on board the ship they have captured, but I bring them home at nightfall, larking and tumbling over each other like happy little boyscouts at play, yet obedient to every order to "concentrate" for any purpose Mr. Bennett or I may wish.

"A Sunday well spent
Means a week of content."

That is, of course, a Sunday spent with both legs swinging all day over ground where grass or heather grows. I have often known the righteous forsaken and his seed begging for bread, but I never knew a man go for an honest day's walk, for whatever distance, great or small, his pair of compasses could measure out in the time, and not have his reward in the repossession of his own soul.

In this medicinal use of Walking, as the Sabbath-day reflection of the tired town worker, companionship is good, and the more friends who join us on the tramp

the merrier. For there is not time, as there is on the longer
holiday or walking tour, for body and mind to attain that
point of training when the higher ecstasies of Walking
are felt through the whole being, those joys that crave
silence and solitude. And indeed, on these humbler occasions, the first half of the day's walk, before the Human
Machine has recovered its tone, may be dreary enough
without the laughter of good company, ringing round
the interchange of genial and irresponsible verdicts on the
topics of the day. For this reason informal Walking socie-
ties should be formed among friends in towns, for week-
end or Sabbath walks in the neighbouring country. I never
get better talk than in these moving Parliaments, and good
talk is itself something.

But here I am reminded of a shrewd criticism directed
against such talking patrols by a good walker who has
written a book on Walking.[1] "In such a case," writes Mr.
Sidgwick — "in such a case walking goes by the board;
the company either loiters" [it depends who is leading]
"and trails in clenched controversy" [then the trailers
must be left behind without pity] "or, what is worse sac-
rilege, strides blindly across country like a herd of animals,
recking little of whence they come or whither they are
going, desecrating the face of nature with sophism and
inference and authority, and regurgitated Blue Book."
[A palpable hit!] "At the end of such a day what have
they profited? Their gross and perishable physical frames
may have been refreshed: their less gross but equally

[1] Sidgwick, *Walking Essays,* pp. 10-11.

perishable minds may have been exercised: but what of their immortal being? It has been starved between the blind swing of the legs below and the fruitless flickering of the mind above, instead of receiving, through the agency of quiet mind and a co-ordinated body, the gentle nutriment which is its due."

Now this passage shows that the author thoroughly understands the high, ultimate end of Walking, which is indeed something other than to promote talk. But he does not make due allowance for times, seasons, and circumstances. You cannot do much with your "immortal soul" in a day's walk in Surrey between one fortnight's work in London and the next; if "body" can be "refreshed" and "mind exercised," it is as much as can be hoped for. The perfection of Walking, such as Mr. Sidgwick describes in the last sentence quoted, requires longer time, more perfect training, and, for some of us at least, a different kind of scenery. Meanwhile let us have good talk as we tramp the lanes.

Nursery lore tells us that "Charles I. walked and talked: half an hour after his head was cut off." Mr. Sidgwick evidently thinks that it was a case not merely of *post hoc* but *propter hoc,* an example of summary but just punishment. Yet, if I read Cromwell aright, he no less than his royal victim would have talked as he walked. And Cromwell reminds me of Carlyle, who carried the art of "walking and talking" to perfection as one of the highest of human functions. Who does not remember his description of "the sunny summer afternoon" when

he and Irving "walked and talked a good sixteen miles"?
Those who have gone walks with Carlyle tell us that then
most of all the fire kindled. And because he talked well
when he walked with others, he felt and thought all the
more when he walked alone, "given up to his bits of re-
flections in the silence of the moors and hills." He was
alone when he walked his fifty-four miles in the day, from
Muirkirk to Dumfries, "the longest walk I ever made,"
he tells us. Carlyle is in every sense a patron saint of
Walking, and his vote is emphatically given *not* for the
"gospel of silence"!

Though I demand silent walking less, I desire solitary
walking more than Mr. Sidgwick. Silence is not enough,
I must have solitude for the perfect walk, which is very
different from the Sunday tramp. When you are really
walking [1] the presence of a companion, involving such irk-
some considerations as whether the pace suits him, whether
he wishes to go up by the rocks or down by the burn, still
more the haunting fear that he may begin to talk, dis-
turbs the harmony of body, mind, and soul when they
stride along no longer conscious of their separate, jarring
entities, made one together in mystic union with the
earth, with the hills that still beckon, with the sunset that
still shows the tufted moor under foot, with old darkness
and its stars that take you to their breast with rapture
when the hard ringing of heels proclaims that you have
struck the final road.

[1] Is there the same sort of difference between *tramping* and *walking* as
between *paddling* and *rowing, scrambling* and *climbing?*

Yet even in such high hours a companion may be good, if you like him well, if you know that he likes you and the pace, and that he shares your ecstasy of body and mind. Even as I write, memories are whispering at my ear how disloyal I am thus to proclaim only solitary walks as perfect. There comes back to me an evening at the end of a stubborn day, when, full of miles and wine, we two were striding towards San Marino over the crest of a high limestone moor — trodden of old by better men in more desperate mood — one of us stripped to the waist, the warm rain falling on our heads and shoulders, our minds become mere instruments to register the goodness and harmony of things, our bodies an animated part of the earth we trod.

And again from out of the depth of days and nights gone by and forgotten, I have a vision not forgettable of making the steep ascent to Volterra, for the first time, under the circlings of the stars; the smell of unseen almond blossom in the air; the lights of Italy far below us; ancient Tuscany just above us, where we were to sup and sleep guarded by the giant walls. Few went to Volterra then, but years have passed, and now I am glad to think that many go, *faute de mieux,* in motor cars; yet so they cannot hear the silence we heard, or smell the almond blossom we smelt, and if they did they could not feel them as the walker can feel. On that night was companionship near to my heart, as also on the evening when together we lifted the view of distant Trasimene, being full of the wine of Papal Pienza and striding on to a supper washed down by Monte Pulciano, itself drawn straight from its native cellars.

Be not shocked, temperate reader! In Italy wine is not a luxury of doubtful omen, but a necessary part of that good country's food. And if you have walked twenty-five miles and are going on again afterwards, you can imbibe Falstaffian potions and still be as lithe and ready for the field as Prince Hal at Shrewsbury. Remember also that in the Latin village tea is in default. And how could you walk the last ten miles without tea? By a providential ordering, wine in Italy is like tea in England, recuperative and innocent of later reaction. Then, too, there are wines in remote Tuscan villages that a cardinal might envy, wines which travel not, but century after century pour forth their nectar for a little clan of peasants, and for any wise English youth who knows that Italy is to be found scarcely in her picture galleries and not at all in her cosmopolite hotels.

Central Italy is a paradise for the walker. I mean the district between Rome and Bologna, Pisa and Ancona, with Perugia for its headquarters, the place where so many of the walking tours of Umbria, Tuscany, and the Marches can be ended or begun.[1] "The olive-sandalled Apennine" is a land always of great views, and at frequent intervals of enchanting detail. It is a land of hills and mountains, unenclosed, open in all directions to the wanderer at will, unlike some British mountain game preserves. And, even in the plains, the peasant, unlike some south-English farm-

[1] The ordnance maps of Italy can be obtained by previous order at London geographers, time allowed, or else bought in Milan or Rome — and sometimes it is possible to get the local ordnance maps in smaller towns.

ers, never orders you off his ground, not even out of his olive grove or vineyard. Only the vineyards in the suburbs of large towns are concealed, reasonably enough, between high white walls. The peasants are kind and generous to the wayfarer. I walked alone in those parts with great success before I knew more than twenty words of Italian. The pleasure of losing your way on those hills leads to a push over broken ground to a glimmer of light that proves to come from some lonely farmstead, with the family gathered round the burning brands, in honest, cheerful poverty. They will, without bargain or demur, gladly show you the way across the brushwood moor, till the lights of Gubbio are seen beckoning down in the valley underneath. And Italian towns when you enter them, though it be at midnight, are still half awake, and every one volunteers in the search to find you bed and board.

April and May are the best walking months for Italy. Carry water in a flask, for it is sometimes ten miles from one well to the next that you may chance to find. A siesta in the shade for three or four hours in the midday heat, to the tune of cicada and nightingale, is not the least pleasant part of all; and that means early starting and night walking at the end, both very good things. The stars out there rule the sky more than in England, big and lustrous with the honour of having shone upon the ancients and been named by them. On Italian mountain tops we stand on naked, pagan earth, under the heaven of Lucretius:

"Luna, dies, et nox, et noctis signa severa."

The chorus-ending from Aristophanes, raised every night from every ditch that drains into the Mediterranean, hoarse and primæval as the raven's croak, is one of the grandest tunes to walk by. Or on a night in May, one can walk through the too rare Italian forests for an hour on end and never be out of hearing of the nightingale's song.

Once in every man's youth there comes the hour when he must learn, what no one ever yet believed save on the authority of his own experience, that the world was not created to make him happy. In such cases, as in that of Teufelsdröckh, grim Walking's the rule. Every man must once at least in life have the great vision of Earth as Hell. Then, while his soul within him is molten lava that will take some lifelong shape of good or bad when it cools, let him set out and walk, whatever the weather, wherever he is, be it in the depths of London, and let him walk grimly, well if it is by night, to avoid the vulgar sights and faces of men, appearing to him, in his then dæmonic mood, as base beyond all endurance. Let him walk until his flesh curse his spirit for driving it on, and his spirit spend its rage on his flesh in forcing it still pitilessly to sway the legs. Then the fire within him will not turn to soot and choke him, as it chokes those who linger at home with their grief, motionless, between four mean, lifeless walls. The stricken one who has, more wisely, taken to road and field, as he plies his solitary pilgrimage day after day, finds that he has with him a companion with whom he is not ashamed to share his grief, even the Earth he treads, his mother who bore him. At the close of a well-trodden day

grief can have strange visions and find mysterious comforts. Hastening at droop of dusk through some remote
byway never to be found again, a man has known a row
of ancient trees nodding over a high stone wall above a
bank of wet earth, bending down their sighing branches
to him as he hastened past for ever, to whisper that the
place knew it all centuries ago and had always been waiting for him to come by, even thus, for one minute in the
night.

Be grief or joy the companion, in youth and in middle
age, it is only at the end of a long and solitary day's walk
that I have had strange casual moments of mere sight and
feeling more vivid and less forgotten than the human
events of life, moments like those that Wordsworth has
described as his common companions in boyhood, like that
night when he was rowing on Esthwaite, and that day when
he was nutting in the woods. These come to me only after
five-and-twenty miles. To Wordsworth they came more
easily, together with the power of expressing them in
words! Yet even his vision and power were closely connected with his long daily walks. De Quincey tells us: "I
calculate, upon good data, that with these identical legs
Wordsworth must have traversed a distance of 175,000 or
180,000 English miles, a mode of exertion which to him
stood in the stead of alcohol and all stimulants whatsoever
to the animal spirits; to which indeed he was indebted for
a life of unclouded happiness, and we for much of what
is most excellent in his writings."

There are many schools of Walking and none of them

orthodox. One school is that of the road-walkers, the Puritans of the religion. A strain of fine ascetic rigour is in these men, yet they number among them at least two poets.[1] Stevenson is *par excellence* their bard:

"Boldly he sings, to the merry tune he marches."

It is strange that Edward Bowen, who wrote the Harrow songs, left no walking songs, though he himself was the king of the roads. Bowen kept at home what he used to call his "road-map," an index outline of the ordnance survey of our island, ten miles to the inch, on which he marked his walks in red ink. It was the chief pride of his life to cover every part of the map with those red spider webs. With this end in view he sought new ground every holiday, and walked not merely in chosen hill and coast districts but over Britain's dullest plains. He generally kept to the roads, partly in order to cover more ground, partly, I suppose, from preference for the free and steady sway of

---

[1] Of the innumerable poets who were walkers we know too little to judge how many of them were *road*-walkers. Shakespeare, one gathers, preferred the footpath way with stiles to either the high road or the moor. Wordsworth preferred the lower fell tracks, above the high roads and below the tops of the hills. Shelley we can only conceive of as bursting over or through all obstacles cross-country; we know he used to roam at large over Shotover and in the Pisan forest. Coleridge is known to have walked alone over Scafell, but he also seems to have experienced after his own fashion the sensations of night-walking on roads:

> "Like one that on a lonesome road
> Doth walk in fear and dread,
> And having once turned round walks on
> And turns no more his head;
> Because he knows a frightful fiend
> Doth close behind him tread."

There is a "personal note" in that! Keats, Matthew Arnold, and Meredith, there is evidence, were "mixed" walkers—on and off the road.

leg over level surface which attracts Stevenson and all de-
votees of the road. He told me that twenty-five miles was
the least possible distance even for a slack day. He was
certainly one of the Ironsides.

To my thinking, the road-walkers have grasped one part
of the truth. The road is invaluable for pace and swing,
and the ideal walk permits or even requires a smooth surface for some considerable portion of the way. On other
terms it is hard to cover a respectable distance, and the
change of tactile values under foot is agreeable.

But more than that I will not concede: twenty-five or
thirty miles of moor and mountain, of wood and field-
path, is better in every way than five-and-thirty, or even
forty, hammered out on the road. Early in life, no doubt,
a man will test himself at pace walking, and then of course
the road must be kept. Every aspiring Cantab. and Oxon-
ian ought to walk to the Marble Arch at a pace that will
do credit to the College whence he starts at break of day: [1]
the wisdom of our ancestors, surely not by an accident,
fixed those two seats of learning each at the same distance
from London, and at exactly the right distance for a test
walk. And there is a harder test than that: if a man can
walk the eighty miles from St. Mary Oxon. to St. Mary
Cantab. in the twenty-four hours, he wins his place with
Bowen and a very few more.

But it is a great mistake to apply the rules of such test
Walking on roads to the case of ordinary Walking. The

[1] Start at five from Cambridge, and have a second breakfast ordered
beforehand at Royston to be ready at eight.

☆ *68* ☆

secret beauties of Nature are unveiled only to the cross-country walker. Pan would not have appeared to Pheidippides on a road. On the road we never meet the "moving acidents by flood or field": the sudden glory of a woodland glade; the open back-door of the old farmhouse sequestered deep in rural solitude; the cow routed up from meditation behind the stone wall as we scale it suddenly; the deep, slow, south-country stream that we must jump, or wander along to find the bridge; the northern torrent of molten peatbog that we must ford up to the waist, to scramble, glowing warm-cold, up the farther foxglove bank; the autumnal dew on the bracken and the blue straight smoke of the cottage in the still glen at dawn; the rush down the mountain side, hair flying, stones and grouse rising at our feet; and at the bottom the plunge in the pool below the waterfall, in a place so fair that kings should come from afar to bathe therein — yet it is left, year in year out, unvisited save by us and "troops of stars." These, and a thousand other blessed chances of the day, are the heart of Walking, and these are not of the road.

Yet the hard road plays a part in every good walk, generally at the beginning and at the end. Nor must we forget the "soft" road, meditating as it were between his hard artificial brother and wild surrounding nature. The broad grass lanes of the low country, relics of mediæval wayfaring; the green, unfenced moorland road; the derelict road already half gone back to pasture; the common farm track — these and all their kind are a blessing to the walker, to be diligently sought out by help of map [1] and used as long as may be. For they unite the speed and smooth surface of the harder road with much at least of the softness to the foot, the romance and the beauty of cross-country routes.

It is well to seek as much variety as is possible in twelve hours. Road and track, field and wood, mountain, hill, and plain should follow each other in shifting vision. The finest poem on the effect of variation in the day's walk is George Meredith's *The Orchard and the Heath*. Some kinds of country are in themselves a combination of different delights, as for example the sub-Lake district, which walkers often see in Pisgah-view from Bowfell or the Old Man, but too seldom traverse. It is a land, sounding with streams from the higher mountains, itself composed of little hills and tiny plains covered half by hazel woods and heather moors, half by pasture and cornfields; and in the middle of the fields rise lesser islands of rocks and patches of the northern jungle still uncleared. The districts along the foot of mountain ranges are often the most varied in feature and therefore the best for Walking.

Variety, too, can be obtained by losing the way — a half-conscious process, which in a sense can no more be done of deliberate purpose than falling in love. And yet a man can sometimes very wisely let himself drift, either into love, or into the wrong path out walking. There is a joy-

[1] Compass and coloured half-inch Bartholomew is the walker's *vade mecum* in the North; the one-inch ordnance is more desirable for the more enclosed and less hilly south of England.

ous mystery in roaming on, reckless where you are, into what valley, road, or farm chance and the hour is guiding you. If the place is lonely and beautiful, and if you have lost all count of it upon the map, it may seem a fairy glen, a lost piece of old England that no surveyor would find though he searched for it a year. I scarcely know whether most to value this quality of aloofness, and magic in country I have never seen before, and may never see again, or the familiar joys of Walking-grounds where every tree and rock are rooted in the memories that make up my life.

Places where the fairies might still dwell lie for the most part west of Avon. Except the industrial plain of Lancashire the whole West from Cornwall to Carlisle is, when compared to the East of our island, more hilly, more variegated, and more thickly strewn with old houses and scenes unchanged since Tudor times. The Welsh border, on both sides of it, is good ground. If you would walk away for a while out of modern England, back and away for twice two hundred years, arrange so that a long day's tramp may drop you at nightfall off the Black Mountain on to the inn that nestles in the ruined tower of old Llan-thony. Then go on through

> "Clunton and Clunbury, Clungunford and Clun,
>   The quietest places under the sun,"

still sleeping their Saxon sleep, with one drowsy eye open for the "wild Welsh" on the "barren mountains" above. Follow more or less the line of Offa's Dyke, which passes, a disregarded bank, through the remotest loveliness of gorse-covered down and thick trailing vegetation of the valley bottoms. Or if you are more leisurely, stay a week at Wigmore till you know the country round by heart. You will carry away much, among other things considerable scepticism as to the famous sentence at the beginning of the third chapter of Macaulay's *History:* "Could the England of 1685 be, by some magical process, set before our eyes, we should not know one landscape in a hundred, or one building in ten thousand." It is doubtful even now, and I suspect that it was a manifest exaggeration when it was written two generation ago. But Macaulay was not much of a walker across country.[1]

One time with another, I have walked twice at least round the coast of Devon and Cornwall, following for the most part the white stones that mark the coastguard track along the cliff. The joys of this method of proceeding have been celebrated by Leslie Stephen in the paragraph quoted at the opening of this essay. But I note that he used to walk there in the summer, when the heather was "purple." I prefer Easter for that region, because when spring comes to deliver our island, like the Prince of Orange he lands first in the South-west. That is when the gorse first smells warm on the cliff-top. Then, too, is the season of daffodils and primroses, which are as native to the creeks of Devon and Cornwall as the scalded cream itself. When the heather is "purple" I will look for it elsewhere.

[1] Like Shelley, he used to *read* as he walked. I do not think Mr. Sidgwick would permit that!

If the walker seeks variety of bodily motion, other than the run down hill, let him scramble. Scrambling is an integral part of Walking, when the high ground is kept all day in a mountain region. To know and love the texture of rocks we should cling to them; and when mountain-ash or holly, or even the gnarled heather root, has helped us at a pinch, we are thenceforth on terms of affection with all their kind. No one knows how sun and water can make a steep bank of moss smell all ambrosia till he has dug foot, fingers, and face into it in earnest. And you must learn to haul yourself up a rock before you can visit those fern-clad inmost secret places where the Spirit of the Gully dwells.

It may be argued that scrambling and its elder brother climbing are the essence of Walking made perfect. I am not a climber and cannot judge. But I acknowledge in the climber the one person who, upon the whole, has not good reason to envy the walker. On the other hand, those stalwart Britons who, for their country's good, shut themselves up in one flat field all day and play there, surrounded by ropes and a crowd, may keep themselves well and happy, but they are divorced from nature. Shooting does well when it draws out into the heart of nature those who could not otherwise be induced to go there. But shooters may be asked to remember that the moors give as much health and pleasure to others who do not carry guns. They may, by the effort of a very little imagination, perceive that it is not well to instruct their gamekeepers to turn every one off the most beautiful grounds in Britain on those 350 days in the year when they themselves are not shooting. Their actual sport should not be disturbed, but there is no sufficient reason for this dog-in-the-manger policy when they are not using the moors. The closing of moors is a bad habit that is spreading in some places, though I hope it is disappearing in others. It is extraordinary that a man not otherwise selfish should probibit the pleasures of those who delight in the moors for their own sakes, on the offchance that he and his guests may kill another stag, or a dozen more grouse in the year. And in most cases an occasional party on the moor makes no difference to the grouse at all. The Highlands have very largely ceased to belong to Britain on account of the deer, and we are in danger of losing the grouse moors as well. If the Alps were British, they would long ago have been closed on account of the chamois.

The energetic walker can of course in many cases despise notice-boards and avoid gamekeepers on the moors, but I put in this plea on behalf of the majority of holiday-makers, including women and children. One would have thought that mountains as well as seas were a common pleasure-ground. But let us register our thanks to the many who do not close their moors.

And the walker, on his side, has his social duties. He must be careful not to leave gates open, not to break fences, not to walk through hay or crops, and not to be rude to farmers. In the interview, always try to turn away from wrath, and in most cases you will succeed.

A second duty is to burn or bury the fragments that remain from lunch. To find the neighbourhood of a stream-head, on some well-known walking route like Scarfell, littered with soaked paper and the relics of the feast is disgusting to the next party. And this brief act of reverence should never be neglected, even in the most retired nooks of the world. For all nature is sacred, and in England there is none too much of it.

Thirdly, though we should trespass we should trespass only so as to temper law with equity. Private gardens and the immediate neighbourhood of inhabited houses must be avoided or only crossed when there is no fear of being seen. All rules may be thus summed up: "Give no man, woman, or child just reason to complain of your passage."

If I have praised wine in Italy, by how much more shall I praise tea in England! — the charmed cup that prolongs the pleasure of the walk and its actual distance by the last, best spell of miles. Before modern times there was Walking, but not the perfection of Walking, because there was no tea. They of old time said, "The traveller hasteth towards evening," but it was then from fear of robbers and the dark, not from the joy of glad living as with us who swing down the darkling road refreshed by tea. Whey they reached the forest of Arden, Rosalind's spirits and Touchstone's legs were weary — but if only Corin could have produced a pot of tea, they would have walked on singing till they found the Duke at dinner. In that scene Shakespeare put his unerring finger fine on the want of his age — tea for walkers at evening.

Tea is not a native product, but it has become our native drink, procured by our English energy at seafaring and trading, to cheer us with the sober courage that fits us best. No, let the swart Italian crush his grape! But grant to me, ye Muses, for heart's ease, at four o'clock or five, wasp-waisted with hunger and faint with long four miles an hour, to enter the open door of a laneside inn, and ask the jolly hostess if she can give me three boiled eggs with my tea — and let her answer "yes." Then for an hour's perfect rest and recovery, while I draw from my pocket some small, well-thumbed volume, discoloured by many rains and rivers, so that some familiar, immortal spirit may sit beside me at the board. There is true luxury of mind and body! Then on again into the night if it be winter, or into the dusk falling or still but threatened — joyful, a man re-made.

Then is the best yet to come, when the walk is carried on into the night, or into the long, silent, twilight hours which in the northern summer stand in night's place. Whether I am alone or with one fit companion, then most is the quiet soul awake; for then the body, drugged with sheer health, is felt only as a part of the physical nature that surrounds it and to which it is indeed akin; while the mind's sole function is to be conscious of calm delight. Such hours are described in Meredith's *Night Walk:*

"A pride of legs in motion kept
Our spirits to their task meanwhile,
And what was deepest dreaming slept:

The posts that named the swallowed mile;
Beside the straight canal the hut
Abandoned; near the river's source
Its infant chirp; the shortest cut;
The roadway missed were our discourse;
At times dear poets, whom some view
Transcendent or subdued evoked . . .
But most the silences were sweet!"

Indeed the only reason, other than weakness of the flesh, for not always walking until late at night, is the joy of making a leisurely occupation of the hamlet that chance or whim has selected for the night's rest. There is much merit in the stroll after supper, hanging contemplative at sunset over the little bridge, feeling at one equally with the geese there on the common and with the high gods at rest on Olympus. After a day's walk everything has twice its usual value. Food and drink become subjects for epic celebration, worthy of the treatment Homer gave them. Greed is sanctified by hunger and health. And as with food, so with books. Never start on a walking tour without an author whom you love. It is criminal folly to waste your too rare hours of perfect receptiveness on the magazines that you may find cumbering the inn. No one, indeed, wants to read long after a long walk, but for a few minutes, at supper or after it, you may be in the seventh heaven with a scene of *Henry IV.*, a chapter of Carlyle, a dozen "Nays, Sirs" of Dr. Johnson, or your own chosen novelist. Their wit and poetry acquire all the richness of your then condition, and that evening they surpass even their own gracious selves. Then, putting the volume in your pocket, go out, and godlike watch the geese.

On the same principle it is good to take a whole day off in the middle of a walking tour. It is easy to get stale, yet it is a pity to shorten a good walk for fear of being tired next day. One day off in a well-chosen hamlet, in the middle of a week's "hard," is often both necessary to the pleasure of the next three days, and good in itself in the same kind of excellence as that of the evening just described. All day long, as we lie *perdu* in wood or field, we have perfect laziness and perfect health. The body is asleep like a healthy infant — or, if it must be doing for one hour of the blessed day, let it scramble a little; while the power of mind and soul are at their topmost strength and yet are not put forth, save intermittently and casually, like a careless giant's hand. Our modern life requires such days of "anti-worry," and they are only to be obtained in perfection when the body has been walked to a standstill.

George Meredith once said to me that we should "love all changes of weather." That is a true word for walkers. Change in weather should be made as welcome as change in scenery. "Thrice blessed is our sunshine after rain." I love the stillness of dawn, and of noon, and of evening, but I love no less the "winds austere and pure." The fight against fiercer wind and snowstorm is among the higher joys of Walking, and produces in shortest time the state of ecstasy. Meredith himself has described once for all in the *Egoist* the delight of Walking soaked through by rain. Still more in mist upon the mountains, to keep the way, or

☆ *78* ☆

to lose and find it, is one of the great primæval games, though now we play it with map and compass. But do not, in mountain mist, "lose the way" on purpose, as I have recommended to vary the monotony of less exciting walks. I once had eight days' walking alone in the Pyrenees, and on only one half-day saw heaven or earth. Yet I enjoyed that week in the mist, for I was kept at work finding the unseen way through pine forest and gurgling Alp, every bit of instinct and hill-knowledge on the stretch. And that one half-day of sunlight, how I treasured it! When we see the mists sweeping up to play with us as we walk the mountain crests, we should "rejoice," as it was the custom of Cromwell's soldiers to do when they saw the enemy. Listen while you can to the roar of waters from behind the great grey curtain, and look at the torrent at your feet tumbling the rocks down gully and glen, for there will be no such sights and sounds when the mists are withdrawn into their lairs, and the mountain, no longer a giant half seen through clefts of scudding cloud, stands there, from scree-foot to cairn, dwarfed and betrayed by the sun. So let us "love all changes of weather."

I have now set down my own experiences and likings. Let no one be alarmed or angry because his ideas of Walking are different. There is no orthodoxy in Walking. It is a land of many paths and no-paths, where every one goes his own way and is right.

J. BROOKS ATKINSON:
A NOTE ON WALKING

In THE YEARS SINCE DR. TREVEL-
yan's discursion on his excursions was originally pub-
lished, the motor car has completely separated the walkers
from the riders. It is a salutary thing thus to distinguish
virtue from vice for all time; but it lays a new responsi-
bility upon the walkers to conduct themselves nobly in
God's light lest even a suspicion of vice foul their reputations. They cannot be road-walkers now, like Stevenson,
since roads have become arteries — hardened arteries — of
traffic. They are pushed willy-nilly into the hills, meadows
and woods, beyond the clatter and the evil fumes of the
highway. It behooves them, therefore, to assert their virtue
more than ever, to give out the perfume of the mountain
laurel in their reputations. When I see walking-clubs of a
Sunday tearing fiercely across the landscape, consulting
watches and schedules, wrenching lilacs and pussy-willows,
feeding grossly and blowing guttural notes on the bugle, I

cannot help thinking that they are instinctively riders. Their walking is a bastard form of motoring.

I am glad that Dr. Trevelyan does not exclude comradeship from his walking code of honor. That is sound philosophy — other essayists to the contrary notwithstanding. Although Hazlitt and Stevenson renounced companionship they were walking-essayists, it seems to me, rather than virgin walkers. Sterne would not go alone; and Thoreau and Hudson, the princes of walking, cherished such comradeship as they found worthy of high enterprises. That sublime distinction between the worthy and the unworthy, of course, brings us back to the old cleavage between virtue and vice; and unless you be particularly fortunate in your associations, you may still have to go alone in spite of your social impulses. Walking companions, like heroes, are difficult to pluck out of the crowd of acquaintances. Good dispositions, ready wit, friendly conversation serve well enough by the fireside but they prove insufficient in the field. For there you need transcendentalists — nothing less; you need poets, sages, humorists and natural philosophers. "I have met with but one or two persons in the course of my life who understood the art of Walking," said Thoreau sententiously. For my part I have met precisely two. Unless one or the other of them can lay down all his worldly affairs on the instant and put on his walking boots, I resign myself to going alone. For the success of the journey depends not upon the miles covered nor upon the country seen, but the mood engendered out of doors; and the sluggishness latent in what Hudson calls "the town mind" slackens the pace even of the clouds. Resign yourself to an imperfect companion and see how scarce the birds and flowers turn out to be, how heavily the branches droop and how literal the landscape becomes. You see only the facts; and the facts are infernally dull.

To me all forms of walking are closely related — the two miles of city pavement between home and office, the holiday in the country and the long summer excursion. "You cannot do much with your 'immortal soul' in a day's walk in Surrey between one fortnight's work in London," writes Dr. Trevelyan. That is true. And yet, it seems to me, you can do something. Even when I walk to the office in the morning I fancy I have achieved something more abiding than mere physical exercise. The first two blocks take me to the subway entrance. As soon as I have passed that, and have thus voluntarily chosen thirty minutes of walking instead of ten minutes of noisy riding, I feel myself reclaimed from civil activity. From that sense of civil freedom to the Nirvana of vagrancy the path is straight and broad. In taking the first step I have done all that is really essential; I have lost identity in the city, and no one can tell what adventures lie ahead.

Not that the city stroll compares favorably with the summer excursion. With two weeks on your hands and forty pounds on your back you can lose your civil identity completely. You can do more. Especially if you go into the deep woods and take up life where the pioneers and hunters resigned it you will discover new and tougher possibilities within yourself. Those are the journeys by which I set most store year after year. Outwardly they are physical experiences — exhausting and rude, and we childishly dramatize the roughness in them by letting our beards grow and our stockings hang loosely. However, if they were only physical experiences I should not retain them so completely as fine-grained memories of high mountain amphitheatres, of thrush songs at sundown, of thickly-matted spruce groves, of whitened torrents, of tarns hidden in the stunted woods, of rain and sunshine and starlight. For those are the truths we experience, not objectively from a veranda or a lookout tower, but subjectively as truths of which we are a part. Walking has carried us out of ourselves into them.

Like all well-grounded walkers, Dr. Trevelyan is tranquil and tolerant, not to be fretted by a simple difference of opinion. "There is no orthodoxy in walking," he writes at the close. "It is a land of many paths and no-paths, where every one goes his own way and is right." It will not be heterodox, therefore, if in this book I sing in praise of resting. He speaks lovingly of the siesta necessary in Italy — "in the shade for three or four hours in the midday heat, to the tune of cicada and nightingale," and he recommends a day off at midweek. Even in the ineptly-termed "temperate zone" of Eastern North America the siesta is one aspect of what philosophers call "the highest good." No tramping-clubs, I am sure, would legitimatize the inconclusive rambles we set forth as walking, for we are in a manner of speaking sedentary walkers. Whenever the prospect is good we find a place to support our backs and we sit there occasionally for an hour at a time. In the winter we sometimes build a fire at lunchtime, both for warmth and for fascination.

And we are confirmed nappers out of doors — even in January if the air is not too brisk. Two naps in particular I remember as adventures of the spirit, when sleeping, dreaming and waking all seemed to be figures in the same pattern of unreality. One was in a little beach-cove by the Hudson River in September; the other was in March on a beach of Long Island Sound. On both occasions I drifted into slumber so naturally that I could not account for it when I awoke. There was a deeper mystery about the nap on Long Island Sound. Marching along the beach I had been trying to come within binocular-view of the ducks that linger there in the spring—hundreds of scoters, scaup and old squaws — but as I approached they moved imperceptibly, and they were always a half mile away. Then I lay down on the buoyant beach grass and presently it seemed to me that I could speak the duck language and that I was enjoying myself hugely in their company. We were laughing and jesting like tavern-cronies. Just as we were getting on famously I was conscious of waking up. But in a measure my dream had come true. For now the ducks had paddled back in great numbers and they were conversing with a loquacity I had never heard before; they were also diving, preening, sleeping, courting, quite unconscious of themselves and of me. Without changing my position I could now watch them through the binoculars and I saw the patterns of their feathering as never before.

It was a memorable experience, simple yet transcendent. As Dr. Trevelyan says of the one day off, the body was "asleep like a healthy infant while the powers of mind and soul were at their topmost strength"; and I wondered if death might not be a similarly gentle transfusion from dull reality to universal reality, to companionship with spirits denied to us here. There is much to be said for lazy walking.

WILLIAM HAZLITT:

ON GOING A JOURNEY

ONE OF THE PLEASANTEST
things in the world is going a journey; but I like to go by
myself. I can enjoy society in a room; but out of doors,
nature is company enough for me. I am then never less
alone than when alone.

The fields his study, nature was his book.

I cannot see the wit of walking and talking at the same
time. When I am in the country, I wish to vegetate like
the country. I am not for criticizing hedge-rows and black
cattle. I go out of town in order to forget the town and all
that is in it. There are those who for this purpose go to
watering-places, and carry the metropolis with them. I
like more elbow-room, and fewer incumbrances. I like
solitude, when I give myself up to it, for the sake of solitude; nor do I ask for

—— a friend in my retreat,
Whom I may whisper, solitude is sweet.

The soul of a journey is liberty, perfect liberty, to think,
feel, do, just as one pleases. We go a journey chiefly to be
free of all impediments and of all inconveniences; to leave
ourselves behind, much more to get rid of others. It is because I want a little breathing-space to muse on indifferent
matters, where Contemplation

May plume her feathers and let grow her wings,
That in the various bustle of resort
    Were all too ruffled, and sometimes impair'd,

that I absent myself from the town for a while, without feeling at a loss the moment I am left by myself. Instead of a friend in a post-chaise or in a Tilbury, to exchange good things with, and vary the same stale topics over again, for once let me have a truce with impertinence. Give me the clear blue sky over my head, and the green turf beneath my feet, a winding road before me, and a three hours' march to dinner — and then to thinking! It is hard if I cannot start some game on these lone heaths. I laugh, I run, I leap, I sing for joy. From the point of yonder rolling cloud, I plunge into my past being, and revel there, as the sun-burnt Indian plunges headlong into the wave that wafts him to his native shore. Then long-forgotten things, like "sunken wrack and sumless treasuries," burst upon my eager sight, and I begin to feel, think, and be myself again. Instead of an awkward silence, broken by attempts at wit or dull commonplaces, mine is that undisturbed silence of the heart which alone is perfect eloquence. No one like puns, alliterations, antitheses, argument and analysis better than I do; but I sometimes had rather be without them. "Leave, oh, leave me to my repose!" I have just now other business in hand, which would seem idle to you, but is with me "very stuff o' the conscience." Is not this wild rose sweet without a comment? Does not this daisy leap to my heart set in its coat of emerald? Yet if I were to explain to you the circumstance that has so endeared it to me, you would only smile. Had I not better then keep it to myself, and let it serve me to brood over, from here to yonder craggy point, and from thence onward to the far-distant horizon? I should be but bad company all that way, and therefore prefer being alone. I have heard it said that you may, when the moody fit comes on, walk or ride on by yourself, and indulge your reveries. But this looks like a breach of manners, a neglect of others, and you are thinking all the time that you ought to rejoin your party. "Out upon such half-faced fellowship," say I. I like to be either entirely to myself, or entirely at the disposal of others; to talk or be silent, to walk or sit still, to be sociable or solitary. I was pleased with an observation of Mr. Cobbett's, that "he thought it a bad French custom to drink our wine with our meals, and that an Englishman ought to do only one thing at a time." So I cannot talk and think, or indulge in melancholy musing and lively conversation by fits and starts. "Let me have a companion of my way," says Sterne, "were it but to remark how the shadows lengthen as the sun declines." It is beautifully said; but in my opinion, this continual comparing of notes interferes with the involuntary impression of things upon the mind, and hurts the sentiment. If you only hint what you feel in a kind of dumb show, it is insipid: if you have to explain it, it is making a toil of a pleasure. You cannot read the book of nature without being perpetually put to the trouble of transplanting it for the benefit of others. I am for the synthetical method on a journey in preference to the analytical. I am content

to lay in a stock of ideas then, and to examine and anato-
mize them afterwards. I want to see my vague notions float
like the down of the thistle before the breeze, and not to
have them entangled in the briars and thorns of controversy. For once, I like to have it all my own way; and
this is impossible unless you are alone, or in such company as I do not covet. I have no objection to argue a
point with any one for twenty miles of measured road, but
not for pleasure. If you remark the scent of a bean-field
crossing the road, perhaps your fellow-traveler has no
smell. If you point to a distant object, perhaps he is short-
sighted, and has to take out his glass to look at it. There is
a feeling in the air, a tone in the color of a cloud which hits
your fancy, but the effect of which you are unable to account for. There is then no sympathy, but an uneasy craving after it, and a dissatisfaction which pursues you on the
way, and in the end probably produces ill-humor. Now I
never quarrel with myself, and take all my own conclu-
sions for granted till I find it necessary to defend them
against objections. It is not merely that you may not be
of accord on the objects and circumstances that present
themselves before you — these may recall a number of objects, and lead to associations too delicate and refined to
be possibly communicated to others. Yet these I love to
cherish, and sometimes still fondly clutch them, when I
can escape from the throng to do so. To give way to our
feelings before company seems extravagance or affectation;
and, on the other hand, to have to unravel this mystery of
our being at every turn, and to make others take an equal

interest in it (otherwise the end is not answered) is a task to which few are competent. We must "give it an understanding, but no tongue." My old friend Coleridge, however, could do both. He could go on in the most delightful explanatory way over hill and dale a summer's day, and convert a landscape into a didactic poem or a Pindaric ode. "He talked far above singing." If I could so clothe my ideas in sounding and flowing words, I might perhaps wish to have some one with me to admire the swelling theme; or I could be more content, were it possible for me still to hear his echoing voice in the woods of All-Foxden.

There is hardly anything that shows the short-sightedness or capriciousness of the imagination more than traveling does. With change of place we change our ideas; nay, our opinions and feelings. We can by an effort indeed transport ourselves to old and long-forgotten scenes, and then the picture of the mind revives again; but we forget those that we have just left. It seems that we can think but of one place at a time. The canvas of the fancy is but of a certain extent, and if we paint one set of objects upon it, they immediately efface every other. We cannot enlarge our conceptions, we only shift our point of view. The landscape bares its bosom to the enraptured eye, we take our fill of it, and seem as if we could form no other image of beauty or grandeur. We pass on, and think no more of it: the horizon that shuts it from our sight also blots it from our memory like a dream. In traveling through a wild, barren country, I can form no idea of a woody and cultivated one. It appears to me that all the world must be barren, like what I see of it. In the country we forget the town, and in town we despise the country. "Beyond Hyde Park," says Sir Fopling Futter, "all is a desert." All that part of the map that we do not see before us is blank. The world in our conceit of it is not much bigger than a nutshell. It is not one prospect expanded into another, county joined to county, kingdom to kingdom, lands to seas, making an image voluminous and vast; — the mind can form no larger idea of space than the eye can take in at a single glance. The rest is a name written in a map, a calculation of arithmetic. For instance, what is the true signification of that immense mass of territory and population, known by the name of China to us? An inch of pasteboard on a wooden globe, of no more account than a China orange! Things near us are seen of the size of life: things at a distance are diminished to the size of the understanding. We measure the universe by ourselves, and even comprehend the texture of our own being only piecemeal. In this way, however, we remember an infinity of things and places. The mind is like a mechanical instrument that plays a great variety of tunes, but it must play them in succession. One idea recalls another, but it at the same time excludes all others. In trying to renew old recollections, we cannot as it were unfold the whole web of our existence; we must pick out the single threads. So in coming to a place where we have formerly lived, and with which we have intimate associations, every one must have found that the feeling grows more vivid the nearer we approach the spot, from the mere anticipation of the actual impression: we remember circumstances, feelings, persons, faces, names that we had not thought of for years; but for the time all the rest of the world is forgotten!

I have no objection to see ruins, acqueducts, pictures, in company with a friend or a party, but rather the contrary, for the former reason reversed. They are intelligible matters, and will bear talking about. The sentiment here is not silent, but communicable and open to view. Salisbury Plain is barren of criticism, but Stonehenge will bear a discussion antiquarian, picturesque, and philosophical. In setting out on a party of pleasure, the first consideration always is where we shall go to: in taking a solitary ramble, the question is what we shall meet with by the way. "The mind is its own pace"; nor are we anxious to arrive at the end of our journey. I can myself do the honors indifferently well to works of art and curiosity. I once took a party to Oxford with no mean *éclat* — showed them that seat of the Muses at a distance,

> With glistering spires and pinnacles adorn'd—

descanted on the learned air that breathes from the grassy quadrangles and stone walls of halls and cottages — was at home in the Bodleian; and at Blenheim quite superseded the powder Cicerone that attended us, and that pointed in vain with his wand to commonplace beauties in matchless pictures. As another exception to the above reasoning, I should not feel confident in venturing on a journey in a foreign country without a companion. I should want at intervals to hear the sound of my own language. There is an involuntary antipathy in the mind of an Englishman to foreign manners and notions that requires the assistance of social sympathy to carry it off. As the distance from home increases, this relief, which was at first a luxury, becomes a passion and an appetite. A person would almost feel stifled to find himself in the deserts of Arabia without friends and countrymen: there must be allowed to be something in the view of Athens or old Rome that claims the utterance of speech; and I own that the Pyramids are too mighty for any single contemplation. In such situations, so opposite to all one's ordinary train of ideas, one seems a species by one's-self, a limb torn off from society, unless one can meet with instant fellowship and support. Yet I did not feel this want or craving very pressing once, when I first set my foot on the laughing shores of France. Calais was peopled with novelty and delight. The confused, busy murmur of the place was like oil and wine poured into my ears; nor did the Mariners' Hymn, which was sung from the top of an old crazy vessel in the harbor, as the sun went down, send an alien sound into my soul. I only breathed the air of general humanity. I walked over "the vine-covered hills and gay regions of France," erect and satisfied; for the image of man was not cast down and chained to the foot of arbitrary thrones; I was at no loss for language, for that of all the great schools of painting was open to me. The whole is vanished like a shade. Pictures, heroes, glory, freedom, all are fled: nothing remains but the Bourbons and the French people! — There is undoubtedly a sensation in traveling into foreign parts that is to be had nowhere else: but it is more pleasing at the time than lasting. It is too remote from our habitual associations to be a common topic of discourse or reference, and, like a dream or another state of existence, does not piece into our daily modes of life. It is an animated but a momentary hallucination. It demands an effort to exchange our actual for our ideal identity; and to feel the pulse of our old transports revive very keenly, we must "jump" all our present comforts and connections. Our romantic and itinerant character is not to be domesticated. Dr. Johnson remarked how little foreign travel added to the facilities of conversation in those who had been abroad. In fact, the time we have spent there is both delightful, and, in one sense, instructive; but it appears to be cut out of our substantial, downright existence, and never to join kindly on to it. We are not the same, but another, and perhaps more enviable individual, all the time we are out of our own country. We are lost to ourselves, as well as our friends. So the poet somewhat quaintly sings,

> Out of my country and myself I go.

Those who wish to forget painful thoughts, do well to absent themselves for a while from the ties and objects that recall them: but we can be said only to fulfil our destiny in the place that gave us birth. I should on this account like well enough to spend the whole of my life in traveling abroad, if I could anywhere borrow another life to spend afterwards at home!

CHARLES DICKENS:

TRAMPS

THE CHANCE USE OF THE WORD
"Tramp" in my last paper, brought that numerous fraternity so vividly before my mind's eye, that I had no
sooner laid down my pen than a compulsion was upon me
to take it up again, and make notes of the Tramps whom
I perceived on all the summer roads in all directions.

Whenever a tramp sits down to rest by the wayside, he
sits with his legs in a dry ditch; and whenever he goes to
sleep (which is very often indeed), he goes to sleep on his
back. Yonder, by the high road, glaring white in the bright
sunshine, lies, on the dusty bit of turf under the bramble-
bush that fences the coppice from the highway, the tramp
of the order savage, fast asleep. He lies on the broad of his
back, with his face turned up to the sky, and one of his
ragged arms loosely thrown across his face. His bundle
(what can be the contents of that mysterious bundle, to
make it worth his while to carry it about?) is thrown down
beside him, and the waking woman with him sits with her
legs in the ditch, and her back to the road. She wears her
bonnet rakishly perched on the front of her head, to shade
her face from the sun in walking, and she ties her skirts
round her in conventionally tight tramp-fashion with a
sort of apron. You can seldom catch sight of her, resting

☆ *95* ☆

thus, without seeing her in a despondently defiant manner doing something to her hair or her bonnet, and glancing at you between her fingers. She does not often go to sleep herself in the daytime, but will sit for any length of time beside the man. And his slumberous propensities would not seem to be referable to the fatigue of carrying the bundle, for she carries it much oftener and further than he. When they are afoot, you will mostly find him slouching on ahead, in a gruff temper, while she lags heavily behind with the burden. He is given to personally correcting her, too — which phase of his character develops itself oftenest, on benches outside alehouse doors — and she appears to become strongly attached to him for these reasons; it may usually be noticed that when the poor creature has a bruised face, she is the most affectionate. He has no occupation whatever, this order of tramp, and has no object whatever in going anywhere. He will sometimes call himself a brickmaker, or a sawyer, but only when he takes an imaginative flight. He generally represents himself, in a vague way, as looking out for a job of work; but he never did work, he never does, and he never will. It is a favourite fiction with him, however (as if he were the most industrious character on earth), that *you* never work; and as he goes past your garden and sees you looking at your flowers, you will overhear him growl with a strong sense of contrast, "*You* are a lucky hidle devil, *you* are!"

The slinking tramp is of the same hopeless order, and has the same injured conviction on him that you were born to whatever you possess, and never did anything to get it:

but he is of a less audacious disposition. He will stop before your gate, and say to his female companion with an
air of constitutional humility and propitiation — to edify
any one who may be within hearing behind a blind or a
bush — "This is a sweet spot, ain't it? A lovely spot! And I
wonder if they'd give two poor footsore travellers like me
and you, a drop of fresh water out of such a pretty gen-teel
crib? We'd take it very koind on 'em, wouldn't us? Wery
koind, upon my word, us would?" He has a quick sense of
a dog in the vicinity, and will extend his modestly-injured
propitiation to the dog chained up in your yard; remark-
ing, as he slinks at the yard gate, "Ah! You are a foine
breed o' dog, too, and *you* ain't kep for nothink! I'd take
it wery koind o' your master if he'd elp a traveller and his
woife as envies no gentlefolk their good fortun, wi' a bit
o' your broken wittles. He'd never know the want of it,
nor more would you. Don't bark like that, at poor persons
as never done you no arm; the poor is down-trodden and
broke enough without that; O DON'T!" He generally heaves
a prodigious sigh in moving away, and always looks up the
lane and down the lane, and up the road and down the
road, before going on.

Both of these orders of tramp are of a very robust habit;
let the hard-working labourer at whose cottage-door they
prowl and beg, have the ague never so badly, these tramps
are sure to be in good health.

There is another kind of tramp, whom you encounter
this bright summer day — say, on a road with the sea-
breeze making its dust lively, and sails of ships in the blue

distance beyond the slope of Down. As you walk enjoyingly on, you descry in the perspective at the bottom of a steep hill up which your way lies, a figure that appears to be sitting airily on a gate, whistling in a cheerful and disengaged manner. As you approach nearer to it, you observe the figure to slide down from the gate, to desist from whistling, to uncock its hat, to become tender of foot, to depress its head and elevate its shoulders, and to present all the characteristics of profound despondency. Arriving at the bottom of the hill and coming close to the figure, you observe it to be the figure of a shabby young man. He is moving painfully forward, in the direction in which you are going, and his mind is so preoccupied with his misfortunes that he is not aware of your approach until you are close upon him at the hill-foot. When he is aware of you, you discover him to be a remarkably well-behaved young man, and a remarkably well-spoken young man. You know him to be well-behaved, by his respectful manner of touching his hat; you know him to be well-spoken, by his smooth manner of expressing himself. He says in a flowing confidential voice, and without punctuation, "I ask your pardon Sir but if you would excuse the liberty of being so addressed upon the public Iway by one who is almost reduced to rags though it as not always been so and by no fault of his own but through ill elth in his family and many unmerited sufferings it would be a great obligation sir to know the time." You give the well-spoken young man the time. The well-spoken young man, keeping well up with you, resumes: "I am aware sir that it is a liberty

to intrude a further question on a gentleman walking for
his entertainment but might I make so bold as ask the
favour of the way to Dover Sir and about the distance?"
You inform the well-spoken young man that the way to
Dover is straight on, and the distance some eighteen miles.
The well-spoken young man becomes greatly agitated. "In
the condition to which I am reduced," says he, "I could
not ope to reach Dover before dark even if my shoes were
in a state to take me there or my feet were in a state to old
out over the flinty road and were not on the bare ground
of which any gentleman has the means to satisfy himself
by looking Sir may I take the liberty of speaking to you?"
As the well-spoken young man keeps so well up with you
that you can't prevent his taking the liberty of speaking
to you, he goes on, with fluency: "Sir it is not begging that
is my intention for I was brought up by the best of mothers
and begging is not my trade I should not know sir how
to follow it as a trade if such were my shameful wishes for
the best of mothers long taught otherwise and in the best
of omes though now reduced to take the present liberty on
the Iway Sir my business was the law-stationering and I
was favourably known to the Solicitor-General the Attor-
ney-General the majority of the Judges and the ole of the
legal profession but through ill elth in my family and the
treachery of a friend for whom I became security and he
no other than my own wife's brother the brother of my
own wife I was cast forth with my tender partner and three
young children not to beg for I will sooner die of depriva-
tion but to make my way in the seaport town of Dover

where I have a relative in respect not only that will assist me but that would trust me with untold gold Sir in appier times and hare this calamity fell upon me I made for my amusement when I little thought that I should ever need it excepting for my air this" — here the well-spoken young man put his hand into his breast — "this comb! Sir I implore you in the name of charity to purchase a tortoiseshell comb which is a genuine article at any price that your humanity may put upon it and may the blessings of a ouseless family awaiting with beating arts the return of a husband and a father from Dover upon the cold stone seats of London-bridge ever attend you Sir may I take the liberty of speaking to you I implore you to buy this comb!" By this time, being a reasonably good walker, you will have been too much for the well-spoken young man, who will stop short and express his disgust and his want of breath, in a long expectoration, as you leave him behind.

Towards the end of the same walk, on the same bright summer day, at the corner of the next little town or village, you may find another kind of tramp, embodied in the persons of a most exemplary couple whose only improvidence appears to have been, that they spent the last of their little All on soap. They are a man and woman, spotless to behold — John Anderson, with the frost on his short smock-front instead of his "pow" attended by Mrs. Anderson. John is over-ostentations of the frost upon his raiment, and wears a curious and, you would say, an almost unnecessary demonstration of girdle of white linen wound about his waist — a girdle, snowy as Mrs. Anderson's apron.

This cleanliness was the expiring effort of the respectable couple, and nothing then remained to Mr. Anderson but to get chalked upon his spade in snowwhite copy-book characters, HUNGRY! and to sit down here. Yes; one thing more remained to Mr. Anderson — his character; Monarchs could not deprive him of his hard-earned character. Accordingly, as you come up with this spectacle of virtue in distress, Mrs. Anderson rises, and with a decent curtsey presents for your consideration a certificate from a Doctor of Divinity, the reverend the Vicar of Upper Dodgington, who informs his Christian friends and all whom it may concern that the bearers, John Anderson and lawful wife, are persons to whom you cannot be too liberal. This benevolent pastor omitted no work of his hands to fit the good couple out, for with half an eye you can recognise his autograph on the spade.

Another class of tramp is a man, the most valuable part of whose stock-in-trade is a highly perplexed demeanour. He is got up like a countryman, and you will often come upon the poor fellow, while he is endeavouring to decipher the inscription on a milestone — quite a fruitless endeavour, for he cannot read. He asks your pardon, he truly does (he is very slow of speech, this tramp, and he looks in a bewildered way all round the prospect while he talks to you), but all of us shold do as we wold be done by, and he'll take it kind, if you'll put a power man in the right road fur to jine his eldest son as has broke his leg bad in the masoning, and is in this heere Orspit'l as is wrote down by Squire Pouncerby's own hand as wold not tell a lie fur no man. He then produces from under his dark frock (being always very slow and perplexed) a neat but worn old leathern purse, from which he takes a scrap of paper. On this scrap of paper is written, by Squire Pouncerby, of The Grove, "Please to direct the Bearer, a poor but very worthy man, to the Sussex County Hospital, near Brighton" — a matter of some difficulty at the moment, seeing that the request comes suddenly upon you in the depths of Hertfordshire. The more you endeavour to indicate where Brighton is — when you have with the greatest difficulty remembered — the less the devoted father can be made to comprehend, and the more obtusely he stares at the prospect; whereby, being reduced to extremity, you recommend the faithful parent to begin by going to St. Albans, and present him with half-a-crown. It does him good, no doubt, but scarcely helps him forward, since you find him lying drunk that same evening in the wheelwright's sawpit under the shed where the felled trees are, opposite the sign of the Three Jolly Hedgers.

But the most vicious, by far, of all the idle tramps, is the tramp who pretends to have been a gentleman. "Educated," he writes, from the village beer-shop in pale ink of a ferruginous complexion; "educated at Trin. Coll. Cam. — nursed in the lap of affluence — once in my small way the pattron of the Muses," etc. etc. etc. — surely a sympathetic mind will not withhold a trifle, to help him on to the market-town where he thinks of giving a Lecture to the *fruges consumere nati,* on things in general? This shameful creature lolling about hedge tap-rooms in his ragged clothes, now so far from being black that they look as if they never can have been black, is more selfish and insolent than even the savage tramp. He would sponge on the poorest boy for a farthing, and spurn him when he had got it; he would interpose (if he could get anything by it) between the baby and the mother's breast. So much lower than the company he keeps, for his maudlin assumption of being higher, this pitiless rascal blights the summer road as he maunders on between the luxuriant hedges; where (to my thinking) even the wild convolvulus and rose and sweetbriar, are the worse for his going by, and need time to recover from the taint of him in the air.

The young fellows who trudge along barefoot, five or six together, their boots slung over their shoulders, their shabby bundles under their arms, their sticks newly cut from some roadside wood, are not eminently prepossessing, but are much less objectionable. There is a tramp-fellowship among them. They pick one another up at resting stations, and go on in companies. They always go at a fast swing — though they generally limp too — and there is invariably one of the company who has much ado to keep up with the rest. They generally talk about horses, and any other means of locomotion than walking: or, one of the company relates some recent experiences of the road — which are always disputes and difficulties. As for example: "So as I'm a standing at the pump in the market, blest if there don't come up a Beadle, and he ses, 'Mustn't stand here,' he ses. 'Why not?' I ses. 'No beggars allowed in this town,' he ses. 'Who's a beggar?' I ses. 'You are,' he ses.

'Who ever see *me* beg? Did *you?*' I ses. 'Then you're a
tramp,' he ses. 'I'd rather be that than a Beadle,' I ses."
(The company express great approval.) " 'Would you?' he
ses to me. 'Yes, I would,' I ses to him. 'Well,' he ses, 'anyhow, get out of this town.' 'Why, blow your little town!'
I ses, 'who wants to be in it? Wot does your dirty little
town mean by comin' and stickin' itself in the road to anywhere? Why don't you get a shovel and a barrer, and clear
your town out o' people's way?' " (The company expressing the highest approval and laughing aloud, they all go
down the hill.)

Then, there are the tramp handicraft men. Are they not
all over England, in this Midsummer time? Where does
the lark sing, the corn grow, the mill turn, the river run,
and they are not among the lights and shadows, tinker-
ing, chair-mending, umbrella-mending, clock-mending,
knife-grinding? Surely, a pleasant thing, if we were in that
condition of life, to grind our way through Kent, Sussex,
and Surrey. For the worst six weeks or so, we should see
the sparks we ground off, fiery bright against a background
of green wheat and green leaves. A little later, and the ripe
harvest would pale our sparks from red to yellow, until
we got the dark newly-turned land for a background again,
and they were red once more. By that time, we should have
ground our way to the sea cliffs, and the whirr of our
wheel would be lost in the breaking of the waves. Our next
variety in sparks would be derived from contrast with the
gorgeous medley of colours in the autumn woods, and, by
the time we had ground our way round to the heathy lands

between Reigate and Croydon, doing a prosperous stroke of business all along, we should show like a little firework in the light frosty air, and be the next best thing to the blacksmith's forge. Very agreeable, too, to go on a chair-mending tour. What judges we should be of rushes, and how knowingly (with a sheaf and a bottomless chair at our back) we should lounge on bridges, looking over at osier-beds! Among all the innumerable occupations that cannot possibly be transacted without the assistance of lookers-on, chair-mending may take a station in the first rank. When we sat down with our backs against the barn or the public-house, and began to mend, what a sense of popularity would grow upon us! When all the children came to look at us, and the tailor, and the general dealer, and the farmer who had been giving a small order at the little saddler's, and the groom from the great house, and the publican, and even the two skittleplayers (and here note that, howsoever busy all the rest of village human-kind may be, there will always be two people with leisure to play at skittles, wherever village skittles are), what en-couragement would be on us to plait and weave! No one looks at us while we plait and weave these words. Clock-mending again. Except for the slight inconvenience of carrying a clock under our arm, and the monotony of mak-ing the bell go, whenever we came to a human habitation, what a pleasant privilege to give a voice to the dumb cot-tage-clock, and set it talking to the cottage family again. Likewise we foresee great interest in going round by the park plantations, under the overhanging boughs (hares, rabbits, partridges, and pheasants, scudding like mad across and across the chequered ground before us), and so over the park ladder, and through the wood, until we came to the Keeper's lodge. Then, would the Keeper be discoverable at his door, in a deep nest of leaves, smoking his pipe. Then, on our accosting him in the way of our trade, would he call to Mrs. Keeper, respecting "t'ould clock" in the kitchen. Then, would Mrs. Keeper ask us into the lodge, and on due examination we should offer to make a good job of it for eighteenpence; which offer, being accepted, would set us tinkling and clinking among the chubby awe-struck little Keepers for an hour and more. So completely to the family's satisfaction would we achieve our work, that the Keeper would mention how that there was something wrong with the bell of the turret stable-clock up at Hall, and that if we thought good of going up to the housekeeper on the chance of that job too, why he would take us. Then, should we go, among the branching oaks and the deep fern, by silent ways of mystery known to the Keeper, seeing the herd glancing here and there as we went along, until we came to the old Hall, solemn and grand. Under the Terrace Flower Garden, and round by the stables, would the Keeper take us in, and as we passed we should observe how spacious and stately the stables, and how fine the painting of the horses' names over their stalls, and how solitary all: the family being in London. Then, should we find ourselves presented to the housekeeper, sitting, in hushed state, at needlework, in a bay-window looking out upon a mighty grim red-brick quadrangle, guarded by stone lions disrespectfully throwing somersaults over the escutcheons of the noble family. Then, our services accepted and we insinuated with a candle into the stable-turret, we should find it to be a mere question of pendulum, but one that would hold us until dark. Then, should we fall to work, with a general impression of Ghosts being about, and of pictures indoors that of a certainty came out of their frames and "walked," if the family would only own it. Then, should we work and work, until the day gradually turned to dusk, and even until the dusk gradually turned to dark. Our task at length accomplished, we should be taken into an enormous servants' hall, and there regaled with beef and bread, and powerful ale. Then, paid freely, we should be at liberty to go, and should be told by a pointing helper to keep round over yinder by the blasted ash, and so straight through the woods, till we should see the town-lights right before us. Then, feeling lonesome, should we desire upon the whole, that the ash had not been blasted, or that the helper had had the manners not to mention it. However, we should keep on, all right, till suddenly the stable bell would strike ten in the dolefullest way, quite chilling our blood, though we had so lately taught him how to acquit himself. Then, as we went on, should we recall old stories, and dimly consider what it would be most advisable to do, in the event of a tall figure, all in white, with saucer eyes, coming up and saying, "I want you to come to a churchyard and mend a church clock. Follow me!" Then, should we make a burst to get clear of the trees, and should soon find ourselves in the open, with the town-lights bright ahead of us. So should we lie that night at the ancient sign of the Crispin and Crispanus, and rise early next morning to be betimes on tramp again.

Bricklayers often tramp, in twos and threes, lying by night at their "lodges," which are scattered all over the country. Bricklaying is another of the occupations that can by no means be transacted in rural parts, without the assistance of spectators — of as many as can be convened. In thinly-peopled spots, I have known bricklayers on tramp, coming up with bricklayers at work, to be so sensible of the indispensability of lookers-on, that they themselves have sat up in that capacity, and have been unable to subside into the acceptance of a proffered share in the job, for two or three days together. Sometimes the "navvy," on tramp, with an extra pair of half-boots over his shoulder, a bag, a bottle, and a can, will take a similar part in a job of excavation, and will look at it without engaging in it, until all his money is gone. The current of my uncommercial pursuits caused me only last summer to want a little body of workmen for a certain spell of work, in a pleasant part of the country; and I was at one time honoured with the attendance of as many as seven-and-twenty, who were looking at six.

Who can be familiar with any rustic highway in summertime, without storing up knowledge of the many tramps who go from one oasis of town or village to another, to sell a stock in trade, apparently not worth a shilling when sold? Shrimps are a favourite commodity for this kind of speculation, and so are cakes of a soft and spongy character, coupled with Spanish nuts and brandy balls. The stock is carried on the head in a basket, and, between the head and the basket, are the trestles on which the stock is displayed at trading times. Fleet of foot, but a careworn class of tramp this, mostly; with a certain stiffness of neck, occasioned by much anxious balancing of baskets; and also with a long Chinese sort of eye, which an overweighted forehead would seem to have squeezed into that form.

On the hot dusty roads near seaport towns and great rivers, behold the tramping Soldier. And if you should happen never to have asked yourself whether his uniform is suited to his work, perhaps the poor fellow's appearance as he comes distressfully towards you, with his absurdly tight jacket unbuttoned, his neck-gear in his hand, and his legs well chafed by his trousers of baize, may suggest the personal inquiry, how you think *you* would like it. Much better the tramping Sailor, although his cloth is somewhat too thick for land service. But, why the tramping merchant-mate should put on a black velvet waistcoat, for a chalky country in the dog-days, is one of the great secrets of nature that will never be discovered.

I have my eye upon a piece of Kentish road, bordered on either side by a wood, and having on one hand, between the road-dust and the trees, a skirting patch of grass. Wild flowers grow in abundance on this spot, and it lies high and airy, with a distant river stealing steadily away to the ocean, like a man's life. To gain the milestone here, which the moss, primroses, violets, blue-bells, and wild roses,

would soon render illegible but for peering travellers push-
ing them aside with their sticks, you must come up a steep
hill, come which way you may. So, all the tramps with carts
or caravans — the Gipsy-tramp, the Show-tramp, the Cheap
Jack — find it impossible to resist the temptations of the
place, and all turn the horse loose when they come to it,
and boil the pot. Bless the place, I love the ashes of the
vagabond fires that have scorched its grass! What tramp
children do I see here, attired in a handful of rags, making
a gymnasium of the shafts of the cart, making a feather-bed
of the flints and brambles, making a toy of the hobbled old
horse who is not much more like a horse than any cheap
toy would be! Here, do I encounter the cart of mats and
brooms and baskets — with all thoughts of business given
to the evening wind — with the stew made and being
served out — with Cheap Jack and Dear Jill striking soft
music out of the plates that are rattled like warlike cym-
bals when put up for auction at fairs and markets — their
minds so influenced (no doubt) by the melody of the
nightingales as they begin to sing in the woods behind
them, that if I were to propose to deal, they would sell me
anything at cost price. On this hallowed ground has it been
my happy privilege (let me whisper it), to behold the
White-haired Lady with the pink eyes, eating meat-pie
with the Giant: while, by the hedgeside, on the box of
blankets which I knew contained the snakes, were set forth
the cups and saucers and the teapot. It was on an evening
in August, that I chanced upon this ravishing spectacle,
and I noticed that, whereas the Giant reclined half con-

cealed beneath the overhanging boughs and seemed indifferent to Nature, the white hair of the gracious Lady streamed free in the breath of evening, and her pink eyes found pleasure in the landscape. I heard only a single sentence of her uttering, yet it bespoke a talent for modest repartee. The ill-mannered Giant — accursed be his evil race! — had interrupted the Lady in some remark, and, as I passed that enchanted corner of the wood, she gently reproved him, with the words, "Now, Cobby"; — Cobby! so short a name! — "ain't one fool enough to talk at a time?"

Within appropriate distance of this magic ground, though not so near it as that the song trolled from tap or bench at door, can invade its woodland silence, is a little hostelry which no man possessed of a penny was ever known to pass in warm weather. Before its entrance are certain pleasant trimmed limes; likewise a cool well, with so musical a bucket-handle that its fall upon the bucket rim will make a horse prick up his ears and neigh, upon the droughty road half a mile off. This is a house of great resort for hay-making tramps and harvest tramps, insomuch that as they sit within, drinking their mugs of beer, their relinquished scythes and reaping-hooks glare out of the open windows, as if the whole establishment were a family war-coach of Ancient Britons. Later in the season, the whole country-side, for miles and miles, will swarm with hopping tramps. They come in families, men, women, and children, every family provided with a bundle of bedding, an iron pot, a number of babies, and too often with some poor sick creature quite unfit for the rough life, for

☆ *111* ☆

whom they suppose the smell of the fresh hop to be a sovereign remedy. Many of these hoppers are Irish, but many come from London. They crowd all the roads, and camp under all the hedges and on all the scraps of common-land, and live among and upon the hops until they are all picked, and the hop-gardens, so beautiful through the summer, look as if they had been laid waste by an invading army. Then, there is a vast exodus of tramps out of the country; and if you ride or drive round any turn of any road, at more than a foot pace, you will be bewildered to find that you have charged into the bosom of fifty families, and that there are splashing up all around you, in the utmost prodigality of confusion, bundles of bedding, babies, iron pots, and a good-humoured multitude of both sexes and all ages, equally divided between perspiration and intoxication.

— From *The Uncommercial Traveller.*

GEORGE GISSING:

WALKING EXPERIENCES

I~N MY GARRET-DAYS IT WAS~
seldom that I rose early: with the exception of one year —
or the greater part of a twelvemonth — during which I
was regularly up at half-past five for a special reason. I had
undertaken to "coach" a man for the London matricula-
tion; he was in business, and the only time he could con-
veniently give to his studies was before breakfast. I, just
then, had lodgings near Hampstead Road; my pupil lived
at Knightsbridge; I engaged to be with him every morning at half-past six, and the walk, at a brisk pace, took me
just about an hour. At that time I saw no severity in the
arrangement, and I was delighted to earn the modest fee
which enabled me to write all day long without fear of
hunger; but one inconvenience attached to it. I had no
watch, and my only means of knowing the time was to
hear the striking of a clock in the neighborhood. As a
rule, I woke just when I should have done; the clock
struck five, and up I sprang. But occasionally — and this
when the mornings had grown dark — my punctual habit
failed me; I would hear the clock chime some fraction of
the hour, and could not know whether I had awoke too soon
or slept too long. The horror of unpunctuality, which has
always been a craze with me, made it impossible to lie

☆ *113* ☆

waiting; more than once I dressed and went out into the street to discover as best I could what time it was, and one such expedition, I well remember, took place between two and three o'clock on a morning of foggy rain.

It happened now and then that, on reaching the house in Knightsbridge, I was informed that Mr. —— felt too tired to rise. This concerned me little, for it meant no de-duction of fee; I had the two hours' walk, and was all the better for it. Then the appetite with which I sat down to breakfast, whether I had done my coaching or not! Bread and butter and coffee — such coffee! — made the meal, and I ate like a navvy. I was in magnificent spirits. All the way home I had been thinking of my day's work, and the morn-ing brain, clarified and whipped to vigour by the brisk exercise, by that wholesome hunger, wrought its best.

More than once, too, when I was walking London streets by night, penniless and miserable, music from an open window has stayed my step, even as yesterday. Very well can I remember such a moment in Eaton Square, one night when I was going back to Chelsea, tired, hungry, racked by frustrate passions. I had tramped miles and miles, in the hope of wearying myself so that I could sleep and forget. Then came the piano notes — I saw that there was a festival in the house — and for an hour or so I revelled as none of the bidden guests could possibly be doing. And when I reached my poor lodgings, I was no longer envious nor mad with desires, but as I fell asleep

I thanked the unknown mortal who had played for me, and given me peace.

Sometimes I added the labour of a porter to my fasting endured for the sake of books. At the little shop near Portland Road Station I came upon a first edition of Gibbon, the price an absurdity — I think it was a shilling a volume. To possess those clean-paged quartos I would have sold my coat. As it happened, I had not money enough with me, but sufficient at home. I was living at Islington. Having spoken with the bookseller, I walked home, took the cash, walked back again, and — carried the tomes from the west end of Euston Road to a street in Islington far beyond the *Angel*. I did it in two journeys — this being the only time in my life when I thought of Gibbon in avoirdupois. Twice — three times reckoning the walk for the money — did I descend on Euston Road and climb Pentonville on that occasion. Of the season and the weather I have no recollection; my joy in the purchase I had made drove out every other thought. Except, indeed, of the weight. I had infinite energy, but not much muscular strength, and the end of the last journey saw me upon a chair, perspiring, flaccid, aching cxultant!

In this hot weather I like to walk at times amid the full glow of the sun. Our island sun is never hot beyond endurance, and there is a magnificence in the triumph of high summer which exalts one's mind. Among streets it is hard to bear, yet even there, for those who have eyes to see it, the splendour of the sky lends beauty to things in themselves mean or hideous. I remember an August bank-holiday, when, having for some reason to walk across London, I unexpectedly found myself enjoying the strange desertion of great streets, and from that passed to surprise in the sense of something beautiful, a charm in the vulgar vista, in the dull architecture which I had never known. Deep and clear marked shadows, such as one only sees on a few days of summer, are in themselves very impressive, and become more so when they fall upon highways devoid of folk. I remember observing, as something new, the shape of familiar edifices, of spires, monuments. And when at length I sat down somewhere on the Embankment, it was rather to gaze at leisure than to rest, for I felt no weariness, and the sun, still pouring upon me its noontide radiance, seemed to fill my veins with life. . . .

Whilst I was reading this afternoon my thoughts strayed, and I found myself recalling a hillside in Suffolk, where, after a long walk, I rested drowsily one midsummer day twenty years ago. A great longing seized me; I was tempted to set off at once, and find again the spot under the high elm trees, where, as I smoked a delicious pipe, I heard about me the crack, crack, crack of broom-pods bursting in the glorious heat of the noontide sun. Had I acted upon the impulse, what chance was there of my enjoying such another hour as that which my memory cherished? No, no; it is not the *place* that I remember; it is the time of life, the circumstances, the mood, which at that moment fell so happily together. Can I dream that a pipe smoked on that same hillside, under the same glowing sky, would taste as it then did, or bring me the same solace? Would the turf be so soft beneath me? Would the great elm-branches temper so delightfully the noontide rays beating upon me? And, when the hour of rest was over, should I spring to my feet as then I did, eager to put forth my strength again? No, no; what I remember is just one moment of my earlier life, linked by accident with that picture of the Suffolk landscape. The place no longer exists; it never existed save for me. For it is the mind which creates the world about us, and, even though we stand side by side in the same meadow, my eyes will never see what is beheld by yours, my heart will never stir to the emotions with which yours is touched.

— From *The Private Papers of Henry Ryecroft.*

CHRISTOPHER MORLEY:
SAUNTERING

SOME FAMOUS LADY — WHO
was it? — used to say of anyone she richly despised that he
was "a saunterer." I suppose she meant he was a mere trifler,
a lounger, an idle stroller of the streets. It is an ignominious
confession, but I am a confirmed saunterer. I love to be set
down haphazard among unknown byways; to saunter with
open eyes, watching the moods and humors of men, the
shapes of their dwellings, the criss-cross of their streets. It
is an implanted passion that grows keener and keener. The
everlasting lure of round-the-corner, how fascinating it is!

I love city squares. The most interesting persons are always those who have nothing special to do: children,
nurses, policemen, and actors at 11 o'clock in the morning. These are always to be found in the park; by which
I mean not an enormous sector of denatured countryside
with bridle paths, fishponds and sea lions, but some broad
patch of turf in a shabby elbow of the city, striped with
pavements, with plenty of sun-warmed benches and a cast-

iron zouave erected about 1873 to remind one of the hor-
rors of commemorative statuary. Children scuffle to and
fro; dusty men with spiculous chins loll on the seats; the
uncouth and pathetic vibrations of humankind are on
every side.

It is entrancing to walk in such places and catalogue all
that may be seen. I jot down on scraps of paper a list of
all the shops on a side street; the names of tradesmen that
amuse me; the absurd repartees of gutter children. Why?
It amuses me and that is sufficient excuse. From now until the end of time no one else will ever see life with my
eyes, and I mean to make the most of my chance. Just as
Thoreau compiled a Domesday Book and kind of classi-
fied directory of the sights, sounds and scents of Walden
(carefully recording the manners of a sandbank and the
prejudices of a woodlouse or an apple tree) so I love to
annotate the phenomena of the city. I can be as solitary
in a city street as ever Thoreau was in Walden.

And no Walden sky was ever more blue than the roof
of Washington Square this morning. Sitting here reading
Thoreau I am entranced by the mellow flavor of the
young summer. The sun is just goodly enough to set the
being in a gentle toasting muse. The trees confer together
in a sleepy whisper. I have had buckwheat cakes and syrup
for breakfast, and eggs fried both recto and verso; good
foundation for speculation. I puff cigarettes and am at
peace with myself. Many a worthy waif comes to lounge
beside me; he glances at my scuffed boots, my baggy
trousers; he knows me for one of the fraternity. By their

boots ye shall know them. Many of those who have abandoned the race of this world's honors have a shrewdness all
their own. What is it Thoreau says, with his penetrative
truth? — "Sometimes we are inclined to class those who are
once and a half witted with the half witted, because we
appreciate only a third part of their wit." By the time a
man is thirty he should be able to see what life has to
offer, and take what dishes on the menu agree with him
best. That is whole wit, indeed, or wit-and-a-half. And if
he finds his pleasure on a park bench in ragged trousers
let him lounge then, with good heart. I welcome him to
the goodly fellowship of saunterers, an acolyte of the excellent church of the agorolaters!

These meditations are incurred in the ancient and noble
city of Philadelphia, which is a surprisingly large town at
the confluence of the Biddle and Drexel families. It is
wholly surrounded by cricket teams, fox hunters, beagle
packs, and the Pennsylvania Railroad. It has a very large
zoölogical garden, containing carnivora, herbivora, scrap-
pleivora, and a man from New York who was interned
here at the time of the Centennial Exposition in 1876.
The principal manufactures are carpets, life insurance
premiums, and souvenirs of Independence Hall. Philadelphia was the first city to foresee the advantages of a
Federal constitution and oatmeal as a breakfast food.

And as one walks and speculates among all this visible
panorama, beating one's brains to catch some passing snap-
shots of it, watching, listening, imagining, the whole hulla-
baloo becomes extraordinarily precious. The great faulty

hodgepodge of the city, its very pavements and house-corners, becomes vividly dear. One longs to clutch the whole meaning in some sudden embrace — to utter some testament of affection that will speak plain truth. "Friday I tasted life," said Emily Dickinson, the American Blake. "It was a vast morsel." Something of that baffled exultation seizes one in certain moments of strolling, when the afternoon sun streams down Chestnut street on the homeward pressing crowd, or in clear crisp mornings as one walks through Washington Square. Emily utters her prodigious parables in flashing rockets that stream for an instant in the dusk, then break and sink in colored balls. Most of us cannot ejaculate such dazzles of flame. We pick and poke and stumble our thoughts together, catching at a truth and losing it again.

Agreeable vistas reward the eye of the resolute stroller. For instance, that delightful cluster of back gardens, old brick angles, dormer windows and tall chimneys in the block on Orange Street west of Seventh. Orange Street is the little alley just south of Washington Square. In the clean sunlight of a fresh May morning, with masses of green trees and creepers to set off the old ruddy brick, this quaint huddle of buildings composes into a delightful picture that has been perpetuated by the skilful pencil of Frank H. Taylor. A kindly observer in the Dreer seed warehouse, which backs upon Orange Street, noticed me prowling about and offered to take me up in his elevator. From one of the Dreer windows I had a fascinating glimpse down upon these roofs and gardens. One of them is the rear yard of the Italian consulate at 717 Spruce Street. Another is the broader garden of The Catholic Historical Society, in which I noticed with amusement Nicholas Biddle's big stone bathtub sunning itself. Then there is the garden of the adorable little house at 725 Spruce Street, which is particularly interesting because, when seen from the street, it appears to have no front door. The attic window of that house is just our idea of what an attic window ought to be.

A kind of philosophy distills itself in the mind of the saunterer. Painfully tedious as people often are, they have the sublime quality of interesting one. Not merely by what they say, but often by what they don't say. Their eyes — how amazing is the thought of all those millions of betraying windows! How bravely they struggle to express what is in them. A modern essayist has spoken of "the haggard necessities of parlor conversation." But the life of the streets has no such conventions. It is real: it comes hot from the pan. It is as informal, as direct and as unpretentious as the greetings of dogs. It is a never-failing remedy for the blues.

HILAIRE BELLOC:
THE BRIENZER GRAT

THE BRIENZER GRAT IS AN EX-
traordinary thing. It is quite straight; its summits are, of
course, of different heights, but from below they seem
even, like a ridge: and, indeed, the whole mountain is more
like a ridge than any other I have seen. At one end is a peak
called the "Red Horn," the other end falls suddenly above
Interlaken. It is as steep as anything can be short of sheer
rock. There are no precipices on it, though there are nasty
slabs quite high enough to kill a man — I saw several of
three or four hundred feet. It is about five or six thousand
feet high, and it stands right up and along the northern
shore of the lake of Brienz. I began the ascent.

Spongy meads, that soughed under the feet and grew
steeper as one rose, took up the first few hundred feet.
Little rivulets of mere dampness ran in among the under
moss, and such very small hidden flowers as there were
drooped with the surfeit of moisture. The rain was now
indistinguishable from a mist, and indeed I had come so
near to the level belt of cloud, that already its gloom was
exchanged for that diffused light which fills vapours from
within and lends them their mystery. A belt of thick brushwood and low trees lay before me, clinging to the slope,
and as I pushed with great difficulty and many turns to

right and left through its tangle a wisp of cloud enveloped me, and from that time on I was now in, now out, of a deceptive drifting fog, in which it was most difficult to gauge one's progress.

Now and then a higher mass of rock, a peak on the ridge, would show clear through a corridor of cloud and be hidden again; also at times I would stand hesitating before a sharp wall or slab, and wait for a shifting of the fog to make sure of the best way round. I struck what might have been a loose path or perhaps only a gully; lost it again and found it again. In one place I climbed up a jagged surface for fifty feet, only to find when it cleared that it was no part of the general ascent, but a mere obstacle which might have been outflanked. At another time I stopped for a good quarter of an hour at an edge that might have been an indefinite fall of smooth rock, but that turned out to be a short drop, easy for a man, and not much longer than my body. So I went upwards always, drenched and doubting, and not sure of the height I had reached at any time.

At last I came to a place where a smooth stone lay between two pillard monoliths, as though it had been put there for a bench. Though all around me was dense mist, yet I could see above me the vague shape of a summit looming quite near. So I said to myself —

"I will sit here and wait till it grows lighter and clearer, for I must now be within two or three hundred feet of the top of the ridge, and as anything at all may be on the other side, I had best go carefully and knowing my way."

So I sat down facing the way I had to go and looking upwards, till perhaps a movement of the air might show me against a clear sky the line of the ridge, and so let me estimate the work that remained to do. I kept my eyes fixed on the point where I judged the sky-line to lie, lest I should miss some sudden gleam revealing it; and as I sat there I grew mournful and began to consider the folly of climbing this great height on an empty stomach. The soldiers of the Republic fought their battles often before breakfast, but never, I think, without having drunk warm coffee, and no one should attempt great efforts without some such refreshment before starting. Indeed, my fasting, and the rare thin air of the height, the chill and the dampness that had soaked my thin clothes through and through, quite lowered my blood and left it *piano,* whimpering, and irresolute. I shivered and demanded the sun.

Then I bethought me of the hunk of bread I had stolen, and pulling it out of my haversack I began to munch that ungrateful breakfast. It was hard and stale, and gave me little sustenance; I still gazed upwards into the uniform meaningless light fog, looking for the ridge.

Suddenly, with no warning to prepare the mind, a faint but distinct wind blew upon me, the mist rose in a wreath backward and upward, and I was looking through clear immensity, not at any ridge, but over an awful gulf at great white fields of death. The Alps were right upon me and before me, overwhelming and commanding empty downward distances of air. Between them and me was a narrow dreadful space of nothingness and silence, and a sheer mile below us both, a floor to that prodigious hollow, lay the little lake.

My stone had not been a halting-place at all, but was itself the summit of the ridge, and those two rocks on either side of it framed a notch upon the very edge and sky-line of the high hills of Brienz.

Surprise and wonder had not time to form in my spirit before both were swallowed up by fear. The proximity of that immense wall of cold, the Alps, seen thus full from the level of its middle height and comprehended as it can-not be from the depths; its suggestion of something never changing throughout eternity — yet dead — was a threat to the eager mind. They, the vast Alps, all wrapped round in ice, frozen, and their immobility enhanced by the delicate, roaming veils which (as from an attraction) hovered in their hollows, seemed to halt the process of living. And the living soul whom they thus perturbed was supported by no companionship. There were no trees or blades of grass around me, only the uneven and primal stones of that height. There were no birds in the gulf; there was no sound. And the whiteness of the glaciers, the blackness of the snow-streaked rocks beyond, was glistening and un-softened. There had come something evil into their sub-limity. I was afraid.

Nor could I bear to look downwards. The slope was in no way a danger. A man could walk up it without often using his hands, and a man could go down it slowly with-out any direct fall, though here and there he would have to turn round at each dip or step and hold with his hands and feel a little for his foothold. I suppose the general slope, down, down, to where the green began was not sixty degrees, but have you ever tried looking down five thousand feet at sixty degrees? It drags the mind after it, and I could not bear to begin the descent.

However, I reasoned with myself. I said to myself that a man should only be afraid of real dangers. That nightmare was not for the daylight. That there was now no mist, but a warm sun. Then choosing a gully where water sometimes ran, but now dry, I warily began to descend, using my staff and leaning well backwards.

There was this disturbing thing about the gully, that it went in steps, and before each step one saw the sky just a yard or two ahead: one lost the comforting sight of earth. One knew of course that it would only be a little drop, and that the slope would begin again, but it disturbed one. And it is a trial to drop or clamber down, say fourteen or fifteen feet, sometimes twenty, and then to find no flat foothold but that eternal steep beginning again.

I went very slowly. When I was about half-way down and had come to a place where a shoulder of heaped rock stood on my left and where little parallel ledges led up to it, having grown accustomed to the descent and easier in my mind, I sat down on a slab and drew imperfectly the things I saw: the lake below me, the first forests clinging to the foot of the Alps beyond, their higher slopes of snow, and the clouds that had now begun to gather round them and that altogether hid the last third of their enormous height.

Then I saw a steamer on the lake. I felt in touch with men. The slope grew easier. I snapped my fingers at the great devils that haunt high mountains. I sniffed the gross and comfortable air of the lower valleys. I entered the belt of wood and was soon going quite a pace through the trees, for I had found a path, and was now able to sing. So I did.

At last I saw through the trunks, but a few hundred feet below me, the highroad that skirts the lake. I left the path and scrambled straight down to it. I came to a wall which I climbed, and found myself in somebody's garden. Crossing this and admiring its wealth and order (I was careful not to walk on the lawns), I opened a little private gate and came on to the road, and from there to Brienz was but a short way along a fine hard surface in a hot morning sun, with the gentle lake on my right hand not five yards away, and with delightful trees upon my left, caressing and sometimes even covering me with their shade.

I was therefore dry, ready, and contented when I entered by mid-morning the curious town of Brienz, which is all one long street, and of which the population is Protestant. I say dry, ready, and contented; dry in my clothes, ready for food, contented with men and nature. But as I entered I squinted up that interminable slope, I saw the fog wreathing again along the ridge so infinitely above me, and I considered myself a fool to have crossed the Brienzer Grat without breakfast. But I could get no one in Brienz to agree with me, because no one thought I had done it, though several people there could talk French.

— From *The Path to Rome.*

☆ *128* ☆

HENRY DAVID THOREAU:
WALKING

I WISH TO SPEAK A WORD FOR
Nature, for absolute freedom and wildness, as contrasted
with a freedom and culture merely civil—to regard man
as an inhabitant, or a part and parcel of Nature, rather
than a member of society. I wish to make an extreme statement, if so I may make an emphatic one, for there are
enough champions of civilization: the minister and the
school committee and every one of you will take care of
that.

I have met with but one or two persons in the course
of my life who understood the art of Walking, that is, of
taking walks—who had a genius, so to speak, for *sauntering*: which word is beautifully derived "from idle people
who roved about the country, in the Middle Ages, and
asked charity, under pretense of going *à la Sainte Terre*,"
to the Holy Land, till the children exclaimed, "There goes
a *Sainte-Terrer*," a Saunterer, a Holy-Lander. They who
never go to the Holy Land in their walks, as they pretend,
are indeed mere idlers and vagabonds; but they who do
go there are saunterers in the good sense, such as I mean.
Some, however, would derive the word from *sans terre*,
without land or home, which, therefore, in the good sense,

will mean, having no particular home, but equally at home everywhere. For this is the secret of successful sauntering. He who sits still in a house all the time may be the greatest vagrant of all; but the saunterer, in the good sense, is no more vagrant than the meandering river, which is all the while sedulously seeking the shortest course to the sea. But I prefer the first, which, indeed, is the most probable derivation. For every walk is a sort of crusade, preached by some Peter the Hermit in us, to go forth and reconquer this Holy Land from the hands of the Infidels.

It is true, we are but faint-hearted crusaders, even the walkers, nowadays, who undertake no persevering, never-ending enterprises. Our expeditions are but tours, and come round again at evening to the old hearth-side from which we set out. Half the walk is but retracing our steps. We should go forth on the shortest walk, perchance, in the spirit of undying adventure, never to return—prepared to send back our embalmed hearts only as relics to our desolate kingdoms. If you are ready to leave father and mother, and brother and sister, and wife and child and friends, and never see them again—if you have paid your debts, and made your will, and settled all your affairs, and are a free man, then you are ready for a walk.

To come down to my own experience, my companion and I, for I sometimes have a companion, take pleasure in fancying ourselves knights of a new, or rather an old, order —not Equestrians or Chevaliers, not Ritters or Riders, but Walkers, a still more ancient and honorable class, I trust. The chivalric and heroic spirit which once belonged to the Rider seems now to reside in, or perchance to have subsided into, the Walker—not the Knight, but Walker, Errant. He is a sort of fourth estate, outside of Church and State and People.

We have felt that we almost alone hereabouts practiced this noble art; though, to tell the truth, at least, if their own assertions are to be received, most of my townsmen would fain walk sometimes, as I do, but they cannot. No wealth can buy the requisite leisure, freedom, and independence which are the capital in this profession. It comes only by the grace of God. It requires a direct dispensation from Heaven to become a walker. You must be born into the family of the Walkers. *Ambulator nascitur, non fit.* Some of my townsmen, it is true, can remember and have described to me some walks which they took ten years ago, in which they were so blessed as to lose themselves for half an hour in the woods; but I know very well that they have confined themselves to the highway ever since, whatever pretensions they may make to belong to this select class. No doubt they were elevated for a moment as by the reminiscence of a previous state of existence, when even they were foresters and outlaws.

"When he came to grene wode,
In a mery mornynge,
There he herde the notes small
Of byrdes mery syngynge.

"It is ferre gone, sayd Robyn,
That I was last here;

Me lyste a lytell for to shote
At the donne dere."

I think that I cannot preserve my health and spirits, unless I spend four hours a day at least—and it is commonly more than that—sauntering through the woods and over the hills and fields, absolutely free from all worldly engagements. You may safely say, A penny for your thoughts, or a thousand pounds. When sometimes I am reminded that the mechanics and shopkeepers stay in their shops not only all the forenoon, but all the afternoon too, sitting with crossed legs, so many of them—as if the legs were made to sit upon, and not to stand or walk upon—I think that they deserve some credit for not having all committed suicide long ago.

I, who cannot stay in my chamber for a single day without acquiring some rust, and when sometimes I have stolen forth for a walk at the eleventh hour or four o'clock in the afternoon, too late to redeem the day, when the shades of night were already beginning to be mingled with the daylight, have felt as if I had committed some sin to be atoned for—I confess that I am astonished at the power of endurance, to say nothing of the moral insensibility, of my neighbors who confine themselves to shops and offices the whole day for weeks and months, aye, and years almost together. I know not what manner of stuff they are of—sitting there now at three o'clock in the afternoon, as if it were three o'clock in the morning. Bonaparte may talk of the three-o'clock-in-the-morning courage, but it is nothing to the courage which can sit down cheerfully at this hour in the afternoon over against one's self whom you have known all the morning, to starve out a garrison to whom you are bound by such strong ties of sympathy. I wonder that about this time, or say between four and five o'clock in the afternoon, too late for the morning papers and too early for the evening ones, there is not a general explosion heard up and down the street, scattering a legion of antiquated and house-bred notions and whims to the four winds for an airing—and so the evil cure itself.

How womankind, who are confined to the house still more than men, stand it I do not know; but I have ground to suspect that most of them do not *stand* it at all. When, early in a summer afternoon, we have been shaking the dust of the village from the skirts of our garments, making haste past those houses with purely Doric or Gothic fronts, which have such an air of repose about them, my companion whispers that probably about these times their occupants are all gone to bed. Then it is that I appreciate the beauty and the glory of architecture, which itself never turns in, but forever stands out and erect, keeping watch over the slumberers.

No doubt temperament, and, above all, age, have a good deal to do with it. As a man grows older, his ability to sit still and follow indoor occupations increases. He grows vespertinal in his habits as the evening of life approaches, till at last he comes forth only just before sundown, and gets all the walk that he requires in half an hour.

But the walking of which I speak has nothing in it akin to taking exercise, as it is called, as the sick take medicine at stated hours—as the swinging of dumbbells or chairs; but is itself the enterprise and adventure of the day. If you would get exercise, go in search of the springs of life. Think of a man's swinging dumbbells for his health, when those springs are bubbling up in far-off pastures unsought by him!

Moreover, you must walk like a camel, which is said to be the only beast which ruminates when walking. When a traveler asked Wordsworth's servant to show him her master's study, she answered, "Here is his library, but his study is out of doors."

Living much out of doors, in the sun and wind, will no doubt produce a certain roughness of character—will cause a thicker cuticle to grow over some of the finer qualities of our nature, as on the face and hands, or as severe manual labor robs the hands of some of their delicacy of touch. So, staying in the house, on the other hand, may produce a softness and smoothness, not to say thinness of skin, accompanied by an increased sensibility to certain impressions. Perhaps we should be more susceptible to some influences important to our intellectual and moral growth if the sun had shone and the wind blown on us a little less; and no doubt it is a nice matter to proportion rightly the thick and thin skin. But methinks that is a scurf that will fall off fast enough—that the natural remedy is to be found in the proportion which the night bears to the day, the winter to the summer, thought to experience. There will be so much the more air and sunshine in our thoughts. The callous palms of the laborer are conversant with finer tissues of self-respect and heroism, whose touch thrills the heart, than the languid fingers of idleness. That is mere sentimentality that lies abed by day and thinks itself white, far from the tan and callus of experience.

When we walk, we naturally go to the fields and woods: what would become of us, if we walked only in a garden or a mall? Even some sects of philosophers have felt the necessity of importing the woods to themselves, since they did not go to the woods. "They planted groves and walks of Platanes," where they took *subdiales ambulationes* in porticos open to the air. Of course, it is of no use to direct our steps to the woods, if they do not carry us thither. I am alarmed when it happens that I have walked a mile into the woods bodily, without getting there in spirit. In my afternoon walk I would fain forget all my morning occupations and my obligations to society. But it sometimes happens that I cannot easily shake off the village. The thought of some work will run in my head and I am not where my body is—I am out of my senses. In my walks I would fain return to my senses. What business have I in the woods, if I am thinking of something out of the woods? I suspect myself, and cannot help a shudder, when I find myself so implicated even in what are called good works—for this may sometimes happen.

My vicinity affords many good walks; and though for so many years I have walked almost every day, and sometimes for several days together, I have not yet exhausted them. An absolutely new prospect is a great happiness, and I can still get this any afternoon. Two or three hours' walking will carry me to as strange a country as I expect ever to see. A single farmhouse which I had not seen before is sometimes as good as the dominions of the King of Dahomey. There is in fact a sort of harmony discoverable between the capabilities of the landscape within a circle of ten miles' radius, or the limits of an afternoon walk, and the threescore years and ten of human life. It will never become quite familiar to you.

Nowadays almost all man's improvements, so called, as the building of houses, and the cutting down of the forest and of all large trees, simply deform the landscape, and make it more and more tame and cheap. A people who would begin by burning the fences and let the forest stand! I saw the fences half consumed, their ends lost in the middle of the prairie, and some worldly miser with a surveyor looking after his bounds, while heaven had taken place around him, and he did not see the angels going to and fro, but was looking for an old posthole in the midst of paradise. I looked again, and saw him standing in the middle of a boggy stygian fen, surrounded by devils, and he had found his bounds without a doubt, three little stones, where a stake had been driven, and, looking nearer, I saw that the Prince of Darkness was his surveyor.

I can easily walk ten, fifteen, twenty, any number of miles, commencing at my own door, without going by any house, without crossing a road except where the fox and the mink do: first along by the river, and then the brook, and then the meadow and the woodside. There are square miles in my vicinity which have no inhabitant. From many a hill I can see civilization and the abodes of man afar. The farmers and their works are scarcely more obvious than woodchucks and their burrows. Man and his affairs, church and state and school, trade and commerce, and manufactures and agriculture, even politics, the most alarming of them all—I am pleased to see how little space they occupy in the landscape. Politics is but a narrow field, and that still narrower highway yonder leads to it. I sometimes direct the traveler thither. If you would go to the political world, follow the great road—follow that marketman, keep his dust in your eyes, and it will lead you straight to it; for it, too, has its place merely, and does not occupy all space. I pass from it as from a beanfield into the forest, and it is forgotten. In one half hour I can walk off to some portion of the earth's surface where a man does not stand from one year's end to another, and there, consequently, politics are not, for they are but as the cigar smoke of a man.

The village is the place to which the roads tend, a sort of expansion of the highway, as a lake of a river. It is the body of which roads are the arms and legs—a trivial or quadrivial place, the thoroughfare and ordinary of travelers. The word is from the Latin *villa*, which together with *via*, a way, or more anciently *ved* and *vella*, Varro derives from *veho*, to carry, because the villa is the place to and from which things are carried. They who got their living by teaming were said *vellaturam facere*. Hence, too, the Latin word *vilis* and our vile; also *villain*. This suggests what kind of degeneracy villagers are liable to. They are wayworn by the travel that goes by and over them, without traveling themselves.

Some do not walk at all; others walk in the highways; a few walk across lots. Roads are made for horses and men of business. I do not travel in them much, comparatively, because I am not in a hurry to get to any tavern or grocery or livery stable or depot to which they lead. I am a good horse to travel, but not from choice a roadster. The landscape-painter uses the figures of men to mark a road. He would not make that use of my figure. I walk out into a Nature such as the old prophets and poets, Menu, Moses, Homer, Chaucer, walked in. You may name it America, but it is not America; neither Americus Vespucius, nor Columbus, nor the rest were the discoverers of it. There is a truer account of it in mythology than in any history of America, so called, that I have seen.

However, there are a few old roads that may be trodden with profit, as if they led somewhere now that they are nearly discontinued. There is the Old Marlborough Road, which does not go to Marlborough now, methinks, unless that is Marlborough where it carries me. I am the bolder to speak of it here, because I presume that there are one or two such roads in every town.

THE OLD MARLBOROUGH ROAD

Where they once dug for money,
But never found any;
Where sometimes Martial Miles
Singly files,
And Elijah Wood,

I fear for no good:
No other man,
Save Elisha Dugan,—
O man of wild habits,
Partridges and rabbits,
Who hast no cares
Only to set snares,
Who liv'st all alone,
Close to the bone,
And where life is sweetest
Constantly eatest.
When the spring stirs my blood
With the instinct to travel
I can get enough gravel
On the Old Marlborough Road.
Nobody repairs it,
For nobody wears it;
It is a living way,
As the Christians say.
Not many there be
Who enter therein,
Only the guests of the
Irishman Quin.
What is it, what is it,
But a direction out there,
And the bare possibility
Of going somewhere?
Great guideboards of stone,
But travelers none;
Cenotaphs of the towns
Named on their crowns.
It is worth going to see
Where you *might* be.

☆ *139* ☆

What king
Did the thing,
I am still wondering;
Set up how or when,
By what selectmen,
Gourgas or Lee,
Clark or Darby?
They're a great endeavor
To be something forever;
Blank tablets of stone,
Where a traveler might groan,
And in one sentence
Grave all that is known;
Which another might read,
In his extreme need.
I know one or two
Lines that would do,
Literature that might stand
All over the land,
Which a man could remember
Till next December,
And read again in the Spring,
After the thawing.
If with fancy unfurled
You leave your abode,
You may go round the world
By the Old Marlborough Road.

At present, in this vicinity, the best part of the land is not private property; the landscape is not owned, and the walker enjoys comparative freedom. But possibly the day will come when it will be partitioned off into so-called pleasure grounds, in which a few will take a narrow and exclusive pleasure only—when fences shall be multiplied, and mantraps and other engines invented to confine men to the *public* road, and walking over the surface of God's earth shall be construed to mean trespassing on some gentleman's grounds. To enjoy a thing exclusively is commonly to exclude yourself from the true enjoyment of it. Let us improve our opportunities, then, before the evil days come.

What is it that makes it so hard sometimes to determine whither we will walk? I believe that there is a subtle magnetism in Nature, which, if we unconsciously yield to it, will direct us aright. It is not indifferent to us which way we walk. There is a right way; but we are very liable from heedlessness and stupidity to take the wrong one. We would fain take that walk, never yet taken by us through this actual world, which is perfectly symbolical of the path which we love to travel in the interior and ideal world; and sometimes, no doubt, we find it difficult to choose our direction, because it does not yet exist distinctly in our idea.

When I go out of the house for a walk, uncertain as yet whither I will bend my steps, and submit myself to my instinct to decide for me, I find, strange and whimsical as it may seem, that I finally and inevitably settle southwest, towards some particular wood or meadow or deserted pasture or hill in that direction. My needle is slow to settle—varies a few degrees, and does not always point due southwest, it is true, and it has good authority for this variation, but it always settles between west and south-southwest. The future lies that way to me, and the earth seems more unexhausted and richer on that side. The outline which would bound my walks would be, not a circle, but a parabola, or rather like one of those cometary orbits which have been thought to be non-returning curves, in this case opening westward, in which my house occupies the place of the sun. I turn round and round irresolute sometimes for a quarter of an hour, until I decide, for a thousandth time, that I will walk into the southwest or west. Eastward I go only by force; but westward I go free. Thither no business leads me. It is hard for me to believe that I shall find fair landscapes or sufficient wildness and freedom behind the eastern horizon. I am not excited by the prospect of a walk thither; but I believe that the forest which I see in the western horizon stretches uninterruptedly towards the setting sun, and there are no towns nor cities in it of enough consequence to disturb me. Let me live where I will, on this side is the city, on that the wilderness, and ever I am leaving the city more and more, and withdrawing into the wilderness. I should not lay so much stress on this fact, if I did not believe that something like this is the prevailing tendency of my countrymen. I must walk toward Oregon, and not toward Europe. And that way the nation is moving, and I may say that mankind progress from east to west. Within a few years we have witnessed the phenomenon of a southeastward migration, in the settlement of Australia; but this affects us as a retrograde movement, and, judging from the moral and physical character of the first generation of Australians, has not yet proved a successful experiment. The eastern Tartars think that there is nothing west beyond Thibet. "The world ends there," say they; "beyond there is nothing but a shoreless sea." It is unmitigated East where they live.

We go eastward to realize history and study the works of art and literature, retracing the steps of the race; we go westward as into the future, with a spirit of enterprise and adventure. The Atlantic is a Lethean stream, in our passage over which we have had an opportunity to forget the Old World and its institutions. If we do not succeed this time, there is perhaps one more chance for the race left before it arrives on the banks of the Styx; and that is in the Lethe of the Pacific, which is three times as wide.

I know not how significant it is, or how far it is an evidence of singularity, that an individual should thus consent in his pettiest walk with the general movement of the race; but I know that something akin to the migratory instinct in birds and quadrupeds—which, in some instances, is known to have affected the squirrel tribe, impelling them to a general and mysterious movement, in which they were seen, say some, crossing the broadest rivers, each on its particular chip, with its tail raised for a sail, and bridging narrower streams with their dead—that something like the *furor* which affects the domestic cattle in the spring, and which is referred to a worm in their tails—affects both nations and individuals, either perennially or from time to time. Not a flock of wild geese cackles over our town, but it to some extent unsettles the value of real estate here, and, if I were a broker, I should probably take that disturbance into account.

> "Than longen folk to gon on pilgrimages,
> And palmeres for to seken strange strondes."

Every sunset which I witness inspires me with the desire to go to a West as distant and as fair as that into which the sun goes down. He appears to migrate westward daily, and tempt us to follow him. He is the Great Western Pioneer whom the nations follow. We dream all night of those mountain-ridges in the horizon, though they may be of vapor only, which were last gilded by his rays. The island of Atlantis, and the islands and gardens of the Hesperides, a sort of terrestrial paradise, appear to have been the Great West of the ancients, enveloped in mystery and poetry. Who has not seen in imagination, when looking into the sunset sky, the gardens of the Hesperides, and the foundation of all those fables?

Columbus felt the westward tendency more strongly than any before. He obeyed it, and found a New World for Castile and Leon. The herd of men in those days scented fresh pastures from afar.

> "And now the sun had stretched out all the hills,
> And now was dropped into the western bay;
> At last *he* rose, and twitched his mantle blue;
> Tomorrow to fresh woods and pastures new."

Where on the globe can there be found an area of equal extent with that occupied by the bulk of our States, so fertile and so rich and varied in its productions, and at the same time so habitable by the European, as this is? Michaux, who knew but part of them, says that "the species of large trees are much more numerous in North America than in Europe; in the United States there are more than one hundred and forty species that exceed thirty feet in height; in France there are but thirty that attain this size." Later botanists more than confirm his observations. Humboldt came to America to realize his youthful dreams of a tropical vegetation, and he beheld it in its greatest perfection in the primitive forests of the Amazon, the most gigantic wilderness on the earth, which he has so eloquently described. The geographer Guyot, himself a European, goes farther—farther than I am ready to follow him; yet not when he says: "As the plant is made for the animal, as the vegetable world is made for the animal world, America is made for the man of the Old World. . . . The man of the Old World sets out upon his way. Leaving the highlands of Asia, he descends from station to station towards Europe. Each of his steps is marked by a new civilization superior to the preceding, by a greater power of development. Arrived at the Atlantic, he pauses on the shore of this unknown ocean, the bounds of which he knows not, and turns upon his footprints for an instant." When he has exhausted the rich soil of Europe, and reinvigorated himself, "then recommences his adventurous career westward as in the earliest ages." So far Guyot.

From this western impulse coming in contact with the

barrier of the Atlantic sprang the commerce and enterprise of modern times. The younger Michaux, in his *Travels West of the Alleghanies in 1802,* says that the common inquiry in the newly settled West was, " 'From what part of the world have you come?' As if these vast and fertile regions would naturally be the place of meeting and common country of all the inhabitants of the globe."

To use an obsolete Latin word, I might say, *Ex Oriente lux; ex Occidente* FRUX. From the East light; from the West fruit.

Sir Francis Head, an English traveler and a Governor-General of Canada, tells us that "in both the northern and southern hemispheres of the New World, Nature has not only outlined her works on a larger scale, but has painted the whole picture with brighter and more costly colors than she used in delineating and in beautifying the Old World. . . . The heavens of America appear infinitely higher, the sky is bluer, the air is fresher, the cold is intenser, the moon looks larger, the stars are brighter, the thunder is louder, the lightning is vivider, the wind is stronger, the rain is heavier, the mountains are higher, the rivers longer, the forests bigger, the plains broader." This statement will do at least to set against Buffon's account of this part of the world and its productions.

Linnaeus said long ago, *"Nescio quae facies* laeta, glabra *plantis Americanis* (I know not what there is of joyous and smooth in the aspect of American plants)": and I think that in this country there are no, or at most very few, *Africanae bestiae,* African beasts, as the Romans called them, and that in this respect also it is peculiarly fitted for the habitation of man. We are told that within three miles of the center of the East Indian city of Singapore, some of the inhabitants are annually carried off by tigers; but the traveler can lie down in the woods at night almost anywhere in North America without fear of wild beasts.

These are encouraging testimonies. If the moon looks larger here than in Europe, probably the sun looks larger also. If the heavens of America appear infinitely higher, and the stars brighter, I trust that these facts are symbolical of the height to which the philosophy and poetry and religion of her inhabitants may one day soar. At length, perchance, the immaterial heaven will appear as much higher to the American mind, and the intimations that star it as much brighter. For I believe that climate does thus react on man—as there is something in the mountain air that feeds the spirit and inspires. Will not man grow to greater perfection intellectually as well as physically under these influences? Or is it unimportant how many foggy days there are in his life? I trust that we shall be more imaginative, that our thoughts will be clearer, fresher, and more ethereal, as our sky—our understanding more comprehensive and broader, like our plains—our intellect generally on a grander scale, like our thunder and lightning, our rivers and mountains and forests—and our hearts shall even correspond in breadth and depth and grandeur to our inland seas. Perchance there will appear to the traveler something, he knows not what, of *laeta* and *glabra,* of joyous and serene, in our very faces. Else to what end does the world go on, and why was America discovered?

To Americans I hardly need to say,—

"Westward the star of empire takes its way."

As a true patriot, I should be ashamed to think that Adam in paradise was more favorably situated on the whole than the backwoodsman in this country.

Our sympathies in Massachusetts are not confined to New England; though we may be estranged from the South, we sympathize with the West. There is the home of the younger sons, as among the Scandinavians they took to the sea for their inheritance. It is too late to be studying Hebrew; it is more important to understand even the slang of today.

Some months ago I went to see a panorama of the Rhine. It was like a dream of the Middle Ages. I floated down its historic stream in something more than imagination, under bridges built by the Romans, and repaired by later heroes, past cities and castles whose very names were music to my ears, and each of which was the subject of a legend. There were Ehrenbreitstein and Rolandseck and Coblentz, which I knew only in history. They were ruins that interested me chiefly. There seemed to come up from its waters and its vine-clad hills and valleys a hushed music as of Crusaders departing for the Holy Land. I floated along under the spell of enchantment, as if I had been transported to an heroic age, and breathed an atmosphere of chivalry.

Soon after, I went to see a panorama of the Mississippi,

and as I worked my way up the river in the light of today, and saw the steamboats wooding up, counted the rising cities, gazed on the fresh ruins of Nauvoo, beheld the Indians moving west across the stream, and, as before I had looked up the Moselle, now looked up the Ohio and the Missouri and heard the legends of Dubuque and of Wenona's cliff—still thinking more of the future than of the past or present—I saw that this was a Rhine stream of a different kind; that the foundations of castles were yet to be laid, and the famous bridges were yet to be thrown over the river; and I felt that *this was the heroic age itself,* though we know it not, for the hero is commonly the simplest and obscurest of men.

The West of which I speak is but another name for the Wild; and what I have been preparing to say is, that in Wildness is the preservation of the World. Every tree sends its fibres forth in search of the Wild. The cities import it at any price. Men plough and sail for it. From the forest and wilderness come the tonics and barks which brace mankind. Our ancestors were savages. The story of Romulus and Remus being suckled by a wolf is not a meaningless fable. The founders of every state which has risen to eminence have drawn their nourishment and vigor from a similar wild source. It was because the children of the Empire were not suckled by the wolf that they were conquered and displaced by the children of the northern forests who were.

I believe in the forest, and in the meadow, and in the

night in which the corn grows. We require an infusion of hemlock-spruce or arbor-vitae in our tea. There is a difference between eating and drinking for strength and from mere gluttony. The Hottentots eagerly devour the marrow of the koodoo and other antelopes raw, as a matter of course. Some of our Northern Indians eat raw the marrow of the Arctic reindeer, as well as the various other parts, including the summits of the antlers, as long as they are soft. And herein, perchance, they have stolen a march on the cooks of Paris. They get what usually goes to feed the fire. This is probably better than stall-fed beef and slaughterhouse pork to make a man of. Give me a wildness whose glance no civilization can endure—as if we lived on the marrow of koodoos devoured raw.

There are some intervals which border the strain of the wood-thrush, to which I would migrate—wild lands where no settler has squatted; to which, methinks, I am already acclimated.

The African hunter Cummings tells us that the skin of the eland, as well as that of most other antelopes just killed, emits the most delicious perfume of trees and grass. I would have every man so much like a wild antelope, so much a part and parcel of Nature, that his very person should thus sweetly advertise our senses of his presence, and remind us of those parts of Nature which he most haunts. I feel no disposition to be satirical, when the trapper's coat emits the odor of musquash even; it is a sweeter scent to me than that which commonly exhales from the merchant's or the scholar's garments. When I go into their wardrobes and handle their vestments, I am reminded of no grassy plains and flowery meads which they have frequented, but of dusty merchants' exchanges and libraries rather.

A tanned skin is something more than respectable, and perhaps olive is a fitter color than white for a man—a denizen of the woods. "The pale white man!" I do not wonder that the African pitied him. Darwin the naturalist says, "A white man bathing by the side of a Tahitian was like a plant bleached by the gardener's art, compared with a fine, dark green one, growing vigorously in the open fields."

Ben Jonson exclaims—

"How near to good is what is fair!"

So I would say—

How near to good is what is *wild!*

Life consists with wildness. The most alive is the wildest. Not yet subdued to man, its presence refreshes him. One who pressed forward incessantly and never rested from his labors, who grew fast and made infinite demands on life, would always find himself in a new country or wilderness, and surrounded by the raw material of life. He would be climbing over the prostrate stems of primitive forest-trees.

Hope and the future for me are not in lawns and cultivated fields, not in towns and cities, but in the impervious and quaking swamps. When, formerly, I have analyzed my partiality for some farm which I had contemplated purchasing, I have frequently found that I was attracted solely by a few square rods of impermeable and unfathomable bog— a natural sink in one corner of it. That was the jewel which dazzled me. I derive more of my subsistence from the swamps which surround my native town than from the cultivated gardens in the village. There are no richer parterres to my eyes than the dense beds of dwarf andromeda (*Cassandra calyculata*) which cover these tender places on the earth's surface. Botany cannot go farther than tell me the names of the shrubs which grow there—the high-blueberry, panicled andromeda, lambkill, azalea, and rhodora—all standing in the quaking sphagnum. I often think that I should like to have my house front on this mass of dull red bushes, omitting other flower plots and borders, transplanted spruce and trim box, even graveled walks—to have this fertile spot under my windows, not a few imported barrow-fulls of soil only to cover the sand which was thrown out in digging the cellar. Why not put my house, my parlor, behind this plot, instead of behind that meager assemblage of curiosities, that poor apology for a Nature and Art, which I call my front yard? It is an effort to clear up and make a decent appearance when the carpenter and mason have departed, though done as much for the passer-by as the dweller within. The most tasteful front-yard fence was never an agreeable object of study to me; the most elaborate ornaments, acorn tops, or what not, soon wearied and disgusted me. Bring your sills up to the very edge of the swamp, then (though it may not be the best place for a dry cellar) , so that there be no access on that side to citizens. Front yards are not made to walk in, but, at most, through, and you could go in the back way.

Yes, though you may think me perverse, if it were proposed to me to dwell in the neighborhood of the most beautiful garden that ever human art contrived, or else of a Dismal Swamp, I should certainly decide for the swamp. How vain, then, have been all your labors, citizens, for me!

My spirits infallibly rise in proportion to the outward dreariness. Give me the ocean, the desert, or the wilderness! In the desert, pure air and solitude compensate for want of moisture and fertility. The traveler Burton says of it: "Your *morale* improves; you become frank and cordial, hospitable and single-minded. . . . In the desert, spirituous liquors excite only disgust. There is a keen enjoyment in a mere animal existence." They who have been traveling long on the steppes of Tartary say: "On re-entering cultivated lands, the agitation, perplexity, and turmoil of civilization oppressed and suffocated us; the air seemed to fail us, and we felt every moment as if about to die of asphyxia." When I would recreate myself, I seek the darkest wood, the thickest and most interminable and, to the citizen, most dismal swamp. I enter a swamp as a sacred place —a *sanctum sanctorum*. There is the strength, the marrow of Nature. The wildwood covers the virgin-mould—and the same soil is good for men and for trees. A man's health requires as many acres of meadow to his prospect as his farm does loads of muck. There are the strong meats on which he feeds. A town is saved, not more by the righteous men in it than by the woods and swamps that surround it. A township where one primitive forest waves above while another primitive forest rots below—such a town is fitted to raise not only corn and potatoes, but poets and philosophers for the coming ages. In such a soil grew Homer and Confucius and the rest, and out of such a wilderness comes the Reformer eating locusts and wild honey.

To preserve wild animals implies generally the creation of a forest for them to dwell in or resort to. So it is with man. A hundred years ago they sold bark in our streets peeled from our own woods. In the very aspect of those primitive and rugged trees there was, methinks, a tanning principle which hardened and consolidated the fibres of men's thoughts. Ah! already I shudder for these comparatively degenerate days of my native village, when you cannot collect a load of bark of good thickness—and we no longer produce tar and turpentine.

The civilized nations—Greece, Rome, England—have been sustained by the primitive forests which anciently rotted where they stand. They survive as long as the soil is not exhausted. Alas for human culture! little is to be expected of a nation, when the vegetable mould is exhausted, and it is compelled to make manure of the bones of its fathers. There the poet sustains himself merely by his own superfluous fat, and the philosopher comes down on his marrowbones.

It is said to be the task of the American "to work the virgin soil," and that "agriculture here already assumes proportions unknown everywhere else." I think that the farmer displaces the Indian even because he redeems the meadow, and so makes himself stronger and in some respects more natural. I was surveying for a man the other day a single straight line one hundred and thirty-two rods long, through a swamp, at whose entrance might have been written the words which Dante read over the entrance to the infernal regions: "Leave all hope, ye that enter"—that is, of ever getting out again; where at one time I saw my employer actually up to his neck and swimming for his life in his property, though it was still winter. He had another similar swamp which I could not survey at all, because it was completely under water, and nevertheless, with regard to a third swamp, which I did *survey* from a distance, he remarked to me, true to his instincts, that he would not part with it for any consideration, on account of the mud which it contained. And that man intends to put a girdling ditch round the whole in the course of forty months, and so redeem it by the magic of his spade. I refer to him only as the type of a class.

The weapons with which we have gained our most important victories, which should be handed down as heirlooms from father to son, are not the sword and the lance, but the bushwack, the turf-cutter, the spade, and the bog-hoe, rusted with the blood of many a meadow, and begrimed with the dust of many a hard-fought field. The very winds blew the Indian's cornfield into the meadow, and pointed out the way which he had not the skill to follow. He had no better implement with which to intrench himself in the land than a clamshell. But the farmer is armed with plough and spade.

In literature it is only the wild that attracts us. Dullness is but another name for tameness. It is the uncivilized free and wild thinking in *Hamlet* and the *Iliad*, in all the Scriptures and Mythologies, not learned in the schools, that delights us. As the wild duck is more swift and beautiful than the tame, so is the wild—the mallard—thought, which 'mid falling dews wings its way above the fens. A truly good book is something as natural, and as unexpectedly and unaccountably fair and perfect, as a wild flower discovered on the prairies of the West or in the jungles of the East. Genius is a light which makes the darkness visible, like the lightning's flash, which perchance shatters the temple of knowledge itself—and not a taper lighted at the hearthstone of the race, which pales before the light of common day.

English literature, from the days of the minstrels to the Lake Poets—Chaucer and Spenser and Milton, and even Shakespeare, included—breathes no quite fresh and, in this sense, wild strain. It is an essentially tame and civilized literature, reflecting Greece and Rome. Her wilderness is a greenwood, her wild man a Robin Hood. There is plenty of genial love of Nature, bu* not so much of Nature herself. Her chronicles inform us when her wild animals, but not when the wild man in her, became extinct.

The science of Humboldt is one thing, poetry is another thing. The poet today, notwithstanding all the discoveries of science, and the accumulated learning of mankind, enjoys no advantage over Homer.

Where is the literature which gives expression to Nature? He would be a poet who could impress the winds and streams into his service, to speak for him; who nailed words to their primitive senses, as farmers drive down stakes in the spring, which the frost has heaved; who derived his words as often as he used them—transplanted them to his page with earth adhering to their roots; whose words were so true and fresh and natural that they would appear to expand like the buds at the approach of spring, though they lay half-smothered between two musty leaves in a library,—aye, to bloom and bear fruit there, after their kind, annually, for the faithful reader, in sympathy with surrounding Nature.

I do not know of any poetry to quote which adequately expresses this yearning for the Wild. Approached from this side, the best poetry is tame. I do not know where to find in any literature, ancient or modern, any account which contents me of that Nature with which even I am acquainted. You will perceive that I demand something which no Augustan nor Elizabethan age, which no *culture,* in short, can give. Mythology comes nearer to it than anything. How much more fertile a Nature, at least, has Grecian mythology its root in than English literature! Mythology is the crop which the Old World bore before its soil was exhausted, before the fancy and imagination were affected with blight; and which it still bears, wherever its pristine vigor is unabated. All other literatures endure only as the elms which overshadow our houses; but this is like the great dragon-tree of the Western Isles, as old as mankind, and, whether that does or not, will endure as long; for the decay of other literatures makes the soil in which it thrives.

The West is preparing to add its fables to those of the East. The valleys of the Ganges, the Nile, and the Rhine having yielded their crop, it remains to be seen what the valleys of the Amazon, the Plate, the Orinoco, the St. Lawrence, and the Mississippi will produce. Perchance, when, in the course of ages, American liberty has become a fiction of the past—as it is to some extent a fiction of the present—the poets of the world will be inspired by American mythology.

The wildest dreams of wild men, even, are not the less true, though they may not recommend themselves to the sense which is most common among Englishmen and Americans today. It is not every truth that recommends itself to the common sense. Nature has a place for the wild clematis as well as for the cabbage. Some expressions of truth are reminiscent—others merely *sensible,* as the phrase is—others prophetic. Some forms of disease, even, may prophesy forms of health. The geologist has discovered that the figures of serpents, griffins, flying dragons, and other fanciful embellishments of heraldry have their prototypes in the forms of fossil species which were extinct before man was created, and hence "indicate a faint and shadowy knowledge of a previous state of organic existence." The Hindoos dreamed that the earth rested on an elephant, and the elephant on a tortoise, and the tortoise on a serpent; and though it may be an unimportant coincidence, it will not be out of place here to state, that a fossile tortoise has lately been discovered in Asia large enough to support an elephant. I confess that I am partial to these wild fancies, which transcend the order of time and development. They are the sublimest recreation of the intellect. The partridge loves peas, but not those that go with her into the pot.

In short, all good things are wild and free. There is something in a strain of music, whether produced by an instrument or by the human voice—take the sound of a bugle in a summer night, for instance—which by its wildness, to speak without satire, reminds me of the cries emitted by wild beasts in their native forests. It is so much of their wildness as I can understand. Give me for my friends and neighbors wild men, not tame ones. The wildness of the savage is but a faint symbol of the awful ferity with which good men and lovers meet.

I love even to see the domestic animals reassert their native rights—any evidence that they have not wholly lost their original wild habits and vigor; as when my neighbor's cow breaks out of her pasture early in the spring and boldly swims the river, a cold, gray tide, twenty-five or thirty rods wide, swollen by the melted snow. It is the buffalo crossing the Mississippi. This exploit confers some dignity on the herd in my eyes—already dignified. The seeds of instinct are preserved under the thick hides of cattle and horses, like seeds in the bowels of the earth, an indefinite period.

Any sportiveness in cattle is unexpected. I saw one day a herd of a dozen bullocks and cows running about and frisking in unwieldy sport, like huge rats, even like kittens. They shook their heads, raised their tails, and rushed up and down a hill, and I perceived by their horns, as well as by their activity, their relation to the deer tribe. But, alas! a sudden loud *Whoa!* would have damped their ardor at once, reduced them from venison to beef, and stiffened their sides and sinews like the locomotive. Who but the Evil One has cried, "Whoa!" to mankind? Indeed, the life of cattle, like that of many men, is but a sort of locomotiveness; they move a side at a time, and man, by his machinery, is meeting the horse and the ox halfway. Whatever part the whip has touched is thenceforth palsied. Who would ever think of a *side* of any of the supple cat tribe, as we speak of a *side* of beef?

I rejoice that horses and steers have to be broken before they can be made the slaves of men, and that men themselves have some wild oats still left to sow before they become submissive members of society. Undoubtedly, all men are not equally fit subjects for civilization; and because the majority, like dogs and sheep, are tame by inherited disposition, this is no reason why the others should have their natures broken that they may be reduced to the same level. Men are in the main alike, but they were made several in order that they might be various. If a low use is to be served, one man will do nearly or quite as well as another; if a high one, individual excellence is to be regarded. Any man can stop a hole to keep the wind away, but no other man could serve so rare a use as the author of this illustration did. Confucius says, "The skins of the tiger and the leopard, when they are tanned, are as the skins of the dog and the sheep tanned." But it is not the part of a true cul-

HENRY DAVID THOREAU : *Walking*

ture to tame tigers, any more than it is to make sheep ferocious; and tanning their skins for shoes is not the best use to which they can be put.

When looking over a list of men's names in a foreign language, as of military officers, or of authors who have written on a particular subject, I am reminded once more that there is nothing in a name. The name Menschikoff, for instance, has nothing in it to my ears more human than a whisker, and it may belong to a rat. As the names of the Poles and Russians are to us, so are ours to them. It is as if they had been named by the child's rigmarole—*Iery wiery ichery van, tittle-tol-tan.* I see in my mind a herd of wild creatures swarming over the earth, and to each the herdsman has affixed some barbarous sound in his own dialect. The names of men are of course as cheap and meaningless as *Bose* and *Tray*, the names of dogs.

Methinks it would be some advantage to philosophy, if men were named merely in the gross, as they are known. It would be necessary only to know the genus and perhaps the race or variety, to know the individual. We are not prepared to believe that every private soldier in a Roman army had a name of his own—because we have not supposed that he had a character of his own.

At present our only true names are nicknames. I knew a boy who, from his peculiar energy, was called "Buster" by his playmates, and this rightly supplanted his Christian name. Some travelers tell us that an Indian had no name given him at first, but earned it, and his name was his fame;

and among some tribes he acquired a new name with every new exploit. It is pitiful when a man bears a name for convenience merely, who has earned neither name nor fame.

I will not allow mere names to make distinctions for me, but still see men in herds for all them. A familiar name cannot make a man less strange to me. It may be given to a savage who retains in secret his own wild title earned in the woods. We have a wild savage in us, and a savage name is perchance somewhere recorded as ours. I see that my neighbor, who bears the familiar epithet William, or Edwin, takes it off with his jacket. It does not adhere to him when asleep or in anger, or aroused by any passion or inspiration. I seem to hear pronounced by some of his kin at such a time his original wild name in some jaw-breaking or else melodious tongue.

Here is this vast, savage, howling mother of ours, Nature, lying all around, with such beauty, and such affection for her children, as the leopard; and yet we are so early weaned from her breast to society, to that culture which is exclusively an interaction of man on man—a sort of breeding in and in, which produces at most a merely English nobility, a civilization destined to have a speedy limit.

In society, in the best institutions of men, it is easy to detect a certain precocity. When we should still be growing children, we are already little men. Give me a culture which imports much muck from the meadows, and deepens the soil—not that which trusts to heating manures, and improved implements and modes of culture only!

Many a poor sore-eyed student that I have heard of

would grow faster, both intellectually and physically, if, instead of sitting up so very late, he honestly slumbered a fool's allowance.

There may be an excess even of informing light. Niepce, a Frenchman, discovered "actinism," that power in the sun's rays which produces a chemical effect; that granite rocks, and stone structures, and statues of metal, "are all alike destructively acted upon during the hours of sunshine, and, but for provisions of Nature no less wonderful, would soon perish under the delicate touch of the most subtile of the agencies of the universe." But he observed that "those bodies which underwent this change during the daylight possessed the power of restoring themselves to their original conditions during the hours of night, when this excitement was no longer influencing them." Hence it has been inferred that "the hours of darkness are as necessary to the inorganic creation as we know night and sleep are to the organic kingdom." Not even does the moon shine every night, but gives place to darkness.

I would not have every man nor every part of a man cultivated, any more than I would have every acre of earth cultivated: part will be tillage, but the greater part will be meadow and forest, not only serving an immediate use, but preparing a mould against a distant future, by the annual decay of the vegetation which it supports.

There are other letters for the child to learn than those which Cadmus invented. The Spaniards have a good term to express this wild and dusky knowledge, *Gramática parda,* tawny grammar, a kind of mother-wit derived from that same leopard to which I have referred.

We have heard of a Society for the Diffusion of Useful Knowledge. It is said that knowledge is power, and the like. Methinks there is equal need of a Society for the Diffusion of Useful Ignorance, which we will call Beautiful Knowledge, a knowledge useful in a higher sense: for what is most of our boasted so-called knowledge but a conceit that we know something, which robs us of the advantage of our actual ignorance? What we call knowledge is often our positive ignorance; ignorance, our negative knowledge. By long years of patient industry and reading of the newspapers—for what are the libraries of science but files of newspapers?—a man accumulates a myriad facts, lays them up in his memory, and then when in some spring of his life he saunters abroad into the Great Fields of thought, he, as it were, goes to grass like a horse and leaves all his harness behind in the stable. I would say to the Society for the Diffusion of Useful Knowledge, sometimes—Go to grass. You have eaten hay long enough. The spring has come with its green crop. The very cows are driven to their country pastures before the end of May; though I have heard of one unnatural farmer who kept his cow in the barn and fed her on hay all the year round. So, frequently, the Society for the Diffusion of Useful Knowledge treats its cattle.

A man's ignorance sometimes is not only useful, but beautiful—while his knowledge, so called, is oftentimes worse than useless, besides being ugly. Which is the best man to deal with—he who knows nothing about a subject, and, what is extremely rare, knows that he knows nothing, or he who really knows something about it, but thinks that he knows all?

My desire for knowledge is intermittent; but my desire to bathe my head in atmospheres unknown to my feet is perennial and constant. The highest that we can attain to is not Knowledge, but Sympathy with Intelligence. I do not know that this higher knowledge amounts to anything more definite than a novel and grand surprise on a sudden revelation of the insufficiency of all that we called Knowledge before—a discovery that there are more things in heaven and earth than are dreamed of in our philosophy. It is the lighting up of the mist by the sun. Man cannot *know* in any higher sense than this, any more than he can look serenely and with impunity in the face of the sun: Ὡς τί νοῶν, οὐ κεῖνον νοήσεις,— "You will not perceive that, as perceiving a particular thing," say the Chaldean Oracles.

There is something servile in the habit of seeking after a law which we may obey. We may study the laws of matter at and for our convenience, but a successful life knows no law. It is an unfortunate discovery certainly, that of a law which binds us where we did not know before that we were bound. Live free, child of the mist—and with respect to knowledge we are all children of the mist. The man who takes the liberty to live is superior to all the laws, by virtue of his relation to the lawmaker. "That is active duty," says the Vishnu Purana, "which is not for our bondage; that is knowledge which is for our liberation: all other duty is

☆ *165* ☆

good only unto weariness; all other knowledge is only the cleverness of an artist."

It is remarkable how few events or crises there are in our histories; how little exercised we have been in our minds; how few experiences we have had. I would fain be assured that I am growing apace and rankly, though my very growth disturb this dull equanimity—though it be with struggle through long, dark, muggy nights or seasons of gloom. It would be well, if all our lives were a divine tragedy even, instead of this trivial comedy or farce. Dante, Bunyan, and others appear to have been exercised in their minds more than we: they were subjected to a kind of culture such as our district schools and colleges do not contemplate. Even Mahomet, though many may scream at his name, had a good deal more to live for, aye, and to die for, than they have commonly.

When, at rare intervals, some thought visits one, as perchance he is walking on a railroad, then indeed the cars go by without his hearing them. But soon, by some inexorable law, our life goes by and the cars return.

"Gentle breeze, that wanderest unseen,
And bendest the thistles round Loira of storms,
Traveler of the windy glens,
Why hast thou left my ear so soon?"

While almost all men feel an attraction drawing them to society, few are attracted strongly to Nature. In their reaction to Nature men appear to me for the most part, notwithstanding their arts, lower than the animals. It is not

HENRY DAVID THOREAU : *Walking*

often a beautiful relation, as in the case of the animals. How little appreciation of the beauty of the landscape there is among us! We have to be told that the Greeks called the world Κόσμος, Beauty, or Order, but we do not see clearly why they did so, and we esteem it at best only a curious philological fact.

For my part, I feel that with regard to Nature I live a sort of border life, on the confines of a world into which I make occasional and transient forays only, and my patriotism and allegiance to the State into whose territories I seem to retreat are those of a mosstrooper. Unto a life which I call natural I would gladly follow even a will-o'-the-wisp through bogs and sloughs unimaginable, but no moon nor firefly has shown me the causeway to it. Nature is a personality so vast and universal that we have never seen one of her features. The walker in the familiar fields which stretch around my native town sometimes finds himself in another land than is described in their owners' deeds, as it were in some faraway field on the confines of the actual Concord, where her jurisdiction ceases, and the idea which the word Concord suggests ceases to be suggested. These farms which I have myself surveyed, these bounds which I have set up, appear dimly still as through a mist; but they have no chemistry to fix them; they fade from the surface of the glass; and the picture which the painter painted stands out dimly from beneath. The world with which we are commonly acquainted leaves no trace, and it will have no anniversary.

I took a walk on Spaulding's Farm the other afternoon.

I saw the setting sun lighting up the opposite side of a stately pine wood. Its golden rays straggled into the aisles of the wood as into some noble hall. I was impressed as if some ancient and altogether admirable and shining family had settled there in that part of the land called Concord, unknown to me—to whom the sun was servant—who had not gone into society in the village—who had not been called on. I saw their park, their pleasure ground, beyond through the wood, in Spaulding's cranberry meadow. The pines furnished them with gables as they grew. Their house was not obvious to vision; the trees grew through it. I do not know whether I heard the sounds of a suppressed hilarity or not. They seemed to recline on the sunbeams. They have sons and daughters. They are quite well. The farmer's cart-path, which leads directly through their hall, does not in the least put them out, as the muddy bottom of a pool is sometimes seen through the reflected skies. They never heard of Spaulding, and do not know that he is their neighbor—notwithstanding I heard him whistle as he drove his team through the house. Nothing can equal the serenity of their lives. Their coat of arms is simply a lichen. I saw it painted on the pines and oaks. Their attics were in the tops of the trees. They are of no politics. There was no noise of labor. I did not perceive that they were weaving or spinning. Yet I did detect, when the wind lulled and hearing was done away, the finest imaginable sweet musical hum—as of a distant hive in May, which perchance was the sound of their thinking. They had no idle thoughts, and no one without could see their work, for their industry was not as in knots and excrescences embayed.

But I find it difficult to remember them. They fade irrevocably out of my mind even now while I speak and endeavor to recall them and recollect myself. It is only after a long and serious effort to recollect my best thoughts that I become again aware of their cohabitancy. If it were not for such families as this, I think I should move out of Concord.

We are accustomed to say in New England that few and fewer pigeons visit us every year. Our forests furnish no mast for them. So, it would seem, few and fewer thoughts visit each growing man from year to year, for the grove in our minds is laid waste—sold to feed unnecessary fires of ambition, or sent to mill, and there is scarcely a twig left for them to perch on. They no longer build nor breed with us. In some more genial season, perchance, a faint shadow flits across the landscape of the mind, cast by the *wings* of some thought in its vernal or autumnal migration, but, looking up, we are unable to detect the substance of the thought itself. Our winged thoughts are turned to poultry. They no longer soar, and they attain only to a Shanghai and Cochin-China grandeur. Those *gra-a-ate thoughts,* those *gra-a-ate men* you hear of!

We hug the earth—how rarely we mount! Methinks we might elevate ourselves a little more. We might climb a tree, at least. I found my account in climbing a tree once.

☆ *169* ☆

It was a tall white pine, on the top of a hill; and though I got well pitched, I was well paid for it, for I discovered new mountains in the horizon which I had never seen before—so much more of the earth and the heavens. I might have walked about the foot of the tree for three score years and ten, and yet I certainly should never have seen them. But, above all, I discovered around me—it was near the end of June—on the ends of the topmost branches only, a few minute and delicate red conelike blossoms, the fertile flower of the white pine looking heavenward. I carried straightway to the village the topmost spire, and showed it to stranger jurymen who walked the streets—for it was court-week—and the farmers and lumber-dealers and wood-choppers and hunters, and not one had ever seen the like before, but they wondered as at a star dropped down. Tell of ancient architects finishing their works on the tops of columns as perfectly as on the lower and more visible parts! Nature has from the first expanded the minute blossoms of the forest only towards the heavens, above men's heads and unobserved by them. We see only the flowers that are under our feet in the meadows. The pines have developed their delicate blossoms on the highest twigs of the wood every summer for ages, as well over the heads of Nature's red children as of her white ones; yet scarcely a farmer or hunter in the land has ever seen them.

Above all, we cannot afford not to live in the present. He is blessed over all mortals who loses no moment of the passing life in remembering the past. Unless our philosophy hears the cock crow in every barnyard within our horizon, it is belated. That sound commonly reminds us that we are growing rusty and antique in our employments and habits of thought. His philosophy comes down to a more recent time than ours. There is something suggested by it that is a newer testament—the gospel according to this moment. He has not fallen astern; he has got up early and kept up early, and to be where he is, is to be in season, in the foremost rank of time. It is an expression of the health and soundness of Nature, a brag for all the world—healthiness as of a spring burst forth, a new fountain of the Muses, to celebrate this last instant of time. Where he lives no fugitive slave laws are passed. Who has not betrayed his master many times since last he heard that note?

The merit of this bird's strain is in its freedom from all plaintiveness. The singer can easily move us to tears or to laughter, but where is he who can excite in us a pure morning joy? When, in doleful dumps, breaking the awful stillness of our wooden sidewalk on a Sunday, or, perchance, a watcher in the house of mourning, I hear a cockerel crow far or near, I think to myself, "There is one of us well, at any rate"—and with a sudden gush return to my senses.

We had a remarkable sunset one day last November. I was walking in a meadow, the source of a small brook, when the sun at last, just before setting, after a cold gray day, reached a clear stratum in the horizon, and the softest, brightest morning sunlight fell on the dry grass and on the stems of the trees in the opposite horizon and on the leaves of the shrub oaks on the hillside, while our shadows stretched long over the meadow eastward, as if we were the only motes in its beams. It was such a light as we could not have imagined a moment before, and the air also was so warm and serene that nothing was wanting to make a paradise of that meadow. When we reflected that this was not a solitary phenomenon, never to happen again, but that it would happen forever and ever an infinite number of evenings, and cheer and reassure the latest child that walked there, it was more glorious still.

The sun sets on some retired meadow, where no house is visible, with all the glory and splendor that it lavishes on cities, and perchance as it has never set before—where there is but a solitary marsh hawk to have his wings gilded by it, or only a musquash looks out from his cabin, and there is some little black-veined brook in the midst of the marsh, just beginning to meander, winding slowly round a decaying stump. We walked in so pure and bright a light, gilding the withered grass and leaves, so softly and serenely bright, I thought I had never bathed in such a golden flood, without a ripple or a murmur to it. The west side of every wood and rising ground gleamed like the boundary of Elysium, and the sun on our backs seemed like a gentle herdsman driving us home at evening.

So we saunter toward the Holy Land, till one day the sun shall shine more brightly than ever he has done, shall perchance shine into our minds and hearts, and light up our whole lives with a great awakening light, as warm and serene and golden as on a bankside in autumn.